UNSOLVED SERIAL KILLERS

10 FRIGHTENING TRUE CRIME CASES OF UNIDENTIFIED SERIAL KILLERS (THE ONES YOU'VE NEVER HEARD OF)

VOLUME 1

Written by

D.R. WERNER

CONTENTS

INTRODUCTION

Jack the Ripper. Ted Bundy. Jeffrey Dahmer. The Son of Sam killer.

Their names have been immortalized in the annals of history as some of the most vicious and shocking serial killers mankind has ever seen. Their brutal methods, their callous wit and determination, and their ability to carry out their activities with reckless abandon has cost the lives of many innocent human beings. Their gruesome kills have been the subject of investigative documentaries, their deep-rooted psychological conditions have been detailed extensively in tell-all books and publications, and their lives have been glamorized in television specials and movies.

You've heard them all. You've seen them all. You've been repulsed by their actions and have heaved a sigh of relief knowing that they've been brought to justice for their crimes.

But what about the others? What about the ones who were never caught? What about the ones everyone has forgotten? Or worse: What if you've never even heard of them?

From the sleepy and rustic small towns of Belgium to the urban smorgasbord of culture in London, from the haunted and desolate open fields of Texas to the vibrant and eclectic utopia of San Francisco, the tales of these unidentified serial killers will chill you to the bone. The fact that the following murderers have yet to be identified will keep you looking over your shoulder for someone who could actually be capable of such crimes.

Immerse yourself in these pages with accounts full of terror and intrigue, racked with unspeakable violence and despicable behavior. The accounts of the witnesses and investigators will leave you in disbelief, and the circumstances leading to the slayings of innocent people will make you think twice about the strangers you meet on the street.

With a passion for true crime and an insatiable curiosity to explore the mind and methods of the serial killer, D.R. Werner is a successful multimedia artist from Dallas, Texas, and an aficionado for frightening mysteries. His research into slayings around the world is fueled by a keen desire to unearth the how's the who's, and the why's behind the most depraved incidents of murder in history, and certainly the ones that have yet to be solved. His insights into the warped minds behind such brutal killings provide the kind of knowledge and expertise that will satiate the curiosity of millions seeking answers to these mysteries.

It is hoped that one day all of the ones that got away will be discovered. But until then, be prepared to enter the lives and exploits of these nameless forces of nature.

And be warned.

1

JACK THE STRIPPER AND THE HAMMERSMITH NUDE MURDERS

Much has been written about the infamous Jack the Ripper, the man solely responsible for a string of brutal killings that terrorized the impoverished area of Whitechapel in London circa 1888. But who could have imagined that the legacy of those murders would haunt London once again almost a century later? This is not the story of Jack the Ripper, the Whitechapel murderer known far and wide and immortalized in popular entertainment, but the story of one you have likely never heard of before.

This is the story of Jack the Stripper and of the Hammersmith Nude Murders.

The Swinging City

1960's London was unrecognizable to those who saw the city being bombed out during World War II. The London that emerged from the ashes brandished a youth that had more freedom and more money in their pockets than ever before. A brand-new era of music, fashion, film-making, advertising and photography had taken the city by storm. Several notable names such as The Rolling Stones, The Who, Jean Shrimpton, and Twiggy became the personification of the Swinging City of London, the Capital of Cool.

The Business Girls

With the emerging generation of affluence, prostitution in London became rampant. Famously, striptease clubs began mushrooming throughout the Soho district, while sex workers plied their trade at the various hotspots frequented by the young and the wealthy. Toward the end of the 1950s, however, new laws made brothels and streetwalkers subject to criminal offenses. Thus, the life of business girls, as it were, became much more challenging. Approaching the police for protection from abuse at the hands of their clients would ultimately lead to the arrests of the women themselves, as they would be charged for soliciting on the streets.

Therefore, most of the sex workers would escort their clients near the banks of the River Thames. This area developed a reputation for being a 'lover's lane,' which made it a hotbed of sexual activity. But, unbeknownst to them, some of the sex workers would be doomed at the very place they would earn their living.

The Origins of the Stripper

The original Jack the Ripper is credited with killing at least five women in London. Not to be outdone, Jack the Stripper is believed to have killed at least six sex workers in London's Hammersmith district. These killings lasted for a year from 1964 to 1965, and it is a widely held belief that the Stripper approached them as a client in order to coax them into taking him somewhere private. But the Stripper had far more gruesome designs on his mind as he subjected the women to his vicious wrath.

His violent murders even inspired the slayings of several other sex workers in London, as there was a prevailing resentment among the conservative citizens against them and the youth in general for what they termed as their 'moral depravity.' The police, already indifferent to the street workers' plight, were only brought into action after the gruesome display of vengeance on women became more prominent. A number of suspects emerged, ranging from a security guard, a child killer, and even a former boxing champion.

Although the suspect list has no shortage of names, the fact remains that after all these years there is no conclusive evidence that Jack the Stripper's true identity was ever discovered.

The Victims

The six victims were working girls who operated in London, unaware of the Stripper's actual intentions with them. Times were tough for sex workers, and due to the stringent laws against their profession they had to take on any client they could in order to make ends meet. In the case of the six, it would ultimately cost them their lives. The shared profession of the victims, as well as the macabre fashion in which their bodies were discovered near the River Thames, led to the newspapers coining the name "Jack the Stripper" in their headlines. It was widely believed that the Stripper took a great deal of sadistic pleasure when he killed his victims, grabbing their necks to strangle them right after they performed oral sex on him. Though the police had no leads, they became determined to catch the Stripper when two detective superintendents became part of the manhunt.

The Strippings

Jack the Stripper's modus operandi was believed to be approaching the business girls as a client and strangling them in the middle of committing sexual acts. As his name suggests, his signature was to leave the women completely undressed; however, their clothing was not all he was stripping. Victims were also found with several of their teeth removed, presumably after they had been killed.

Moreover, the Stripper seemed to be interested in females of a certain shorter stature, as the women whom he murdered were all between 5'0" and 5'4". While this had not been obvious in the beginning, it became quite apparent in the killings that followed. Another important clue discovered much later in the investigation was that the victims appeared to have tiny specks of paint on their skin, which led to further speculation about the identity of the Stripper — or at least hinted at his likely day job.

Hannah Tailford

The first known victim of Jack the Stripper was found on February 2, 1964. Her body was discovered in the River Thames on a cold morning near the Hammersmith Bridge. Once identified as Hannah Tailford, it was further found that she had been missing for ten days. According to the investigation,

Tailford's body had been thrown into the water from a quiet spot near Chiswick called Duke's Meadow, a park famous for being a lover's lane — a go-to spot for sex workers to take their clients.

Tailford's body was completely nude, except for her stockings, and her underwear had been forced down her throat as she was strangled to death. Several of her teeth were pulled out after she had been killed and she had some injuries to the head as well. Tragically, while it was known that she left behind two young children, it was later discovered that at the time of her murder Tailford had been pregnant with her third child. Initially, her death was assumed by authorities to be a suicide, despite the glaring and obvious condition of the corpse. This was primarily due to the reputation of the Thames as being an easy suicide spot, as several bodies were pulled out of the river each year.

Born into a mining family in Lancashire, 30-year-old Tailford was a regular business girl working along Bayswater Road. This was a frequent hunting ground for men on the lookout for some action, and Tailford operated with a group of other sex workers in the area. Though the police had dismissed her death as a suicide in the beginning, they would be shaken out of this delusion when another woman's body would be discovered only two months later.

Irene Lockwood

Jack the Stripper had struck again, as the body of 26-year-old Irene Lockwood was discovered on April 8, 1964. Lockwood's corpse was not far from where Hannah Tailford's had been found near the River Thames, along the same stretch near Duke's Meadow. And much like Tailford, Lockwood's body was also completely nude and she had been assaulted before being strangled to death.

But that isn't where the similarities end between the two. Like Tailford, Lockwood was also short at 5'0" and worked as a prostitute on the same stretch of Bayswater Road in West London. Like Tailford, Lockwood had also been assaulted and killed somewhere else before being dumped into the river. And, in the most horrifying detail to emerge, Lockwood was also pregnant. Just like Tailford.

While the police had yet to declare this as the work of a serial killer, the news-hungry press at the time could not bear to miss out on such a viciously sensational story. They were quick to highlight the similarities with the recent murders to the killings in Whitechapel over seven decades ago and gave birth to the legend of "Jack the Stripper." Only then did the police take the matter seriously, as an outcry over the violence against sex workers was beginning to brew, and they were finally able to declare the murders as linked.

But Jack the Stripper was just getting started.

Helen Barthelemy

Even with two murders linked to the characteristics of the modus operandi and the similarities between the victims, the police dragged their feet on declaring this as the work of a serial killer. But two weeks later, Jack the Stripper would ensure his infamy. On April 24, 1964, the body of 22-year-old Helen Barthelemy was found by passersby. Unlike the bodies of Tailford and Lockwood, Barthelemy's corpse was located in a quiet alleyway called Swyncombe Avenue. Nevertheless, it was a stone's throw from the infamous Duke's Meadow, which was enough for the police to formulate a link between the three murders.

Like Tailford and Lockwood, Barthelemy had been strangled and dumped completely nude, with three of her front teeth pulled out: the grotesque signature move of Jack the Stripper. During the autopsy, it was revealed that she had swallowed semen before she died. This led the police to conclude that she had been performing oral sex on her killer, and had been strangled right after.

Known as 'Teddy" on the streets, Barthelemy was a ravishing beauty born in Scotland who had started her career as a striptease performer in Blackpool. Later, she came to work in London in the Soho area which is notorious for its nightlife and opportunities to find sex workers to this day. Her career was short-lived, however, as she became the Stripper's third victim.

But what made her stand out from the rest of the victims was that her body was found away from the river. Because of this, the police were able to uncover a new clue about the identity of the killer. Barthelemy's body had specks of paint all over her skin, the kind used in painting motor vehicles. This led the police to believe that the murderer may have been a paint sprayer by profession.

Mary Fleming

The summer of 1964 was heating up in more ways than one, as the body of 30-year-old Mary Fleming was discovered July 14, 1964, on an open street in Chiswick, just a little distance away from the river. Much like the women before her, Fleming was also of short stature and a prostitute, and her mouth was full of semen which suggested more oral sex. She had been strangled as well, and her front teeth were pulled out afterwards. There were also some paint specks found on Fleming's nude body just like they were on Barthelemy's. The pattern was indeed consistent with the previous killings but this time, the people who had found the body reported a vehicle reversing down the street before they came upon the corpse.

The police were able to determine that the Stripper was storing the bodies somewhere else before discarding them near the Thames, possibly at a vehicle workshop considering the number of paint specks that were found on the corpses. But to what sinister end he was doing this baffled everyone.

Frances Brown

On November 25, 1964, the Stripper's fifth victim was found in a car park near the busy Kensington High Street. At the outset, the 21-year-old Frances Brown was quite unlike the rest of the Stripper's victims. As opposed to a street sex worker, she was a high-class call girl who frequently provided her services to an exclusive clientele. Brown was also quite famous at the time, as she had been involved in a scandalous court trial against a Secretary of State. Her body being discovered marked a departure from the Stripper's usual territory of the Thames River or West London.

Nevertheless, the signature gruesome style of Jack the Stripper was all over the corpse. Brown had been stripped naked and strangled, while also missing a tooth. She was also short in height and had similar paint specks across her skin, much like Barthelemy and Fleming before her. Another breakthrough for the police was that Brown had been last seen alive by a friend a month earlier, on October 23, 1964. The friend, Kim Taylor, had seen the man who had picked Brown up when she saw her last. This proved to be instrumental as her description of the man provided the police with a composite sketch of the suspect and a description of the vehicle he was driving. Based on the description, the car was either a Ford Zephyr or Ford Zodiac, and proved to be somewhat consistent with the report of a vehicle driving off when Mary Fleming's body was found earlier that year.

Bridget "Bridie" O'Hara

The last of The Stripper's known victims was found on February 16, 1965, nearly three months after Frances Brown was found murdered. The body of Bridget O'Hara was discovered close to a shed behind the Heron Trading Estate in West London, just over a year after the first victim, Hannah Tailford, had been found. She was discovered by an electrical fitter who was heading to the estate.

O'Hara's body provided some vital clues to the police with regards to the Stripper's methods. The body was partially mummified which suggested that it had been stored at a warm location. Inside the shed the police found an electrical transformer which proved to be the cause of the body's warmth. There was also a spray paint shop across from the shed, and the specks of paint found on the corpse seemed to come from there.

Born in Dublin, Ireland, Bridget O'Hara had come to London to make a living as a sex worker. Known as 'Bridie,' she had been missing since January 11, 1965. It is likely she had been murdered and kept in storage until she was found by the shed near the estate.

The Others

The modus operandi of Jack The Stripper prompted the police to look into past cases following a similar method. Two other women named Elizabeth Figg and Gwyneth Rees had been strangled to death and found near the Thames. Figg had been killed, and her body was discovered on June 17, 1959, while Rees was found deceased in 1963. Both women were mostly or partially nude, and it may be possible that these were test runs for the Stripper. A total of five unsolved cases dating back to the 1950s were investigated again.

The Investigation

The investigation into the Hammersmith Nude Murders did not yield any conclusive results. Led by Chief Superintendent John Du Rose, roughly 7,000 suspects were brought in for questioning, from which 20 were narrowed down. Ultimately, just three suspects remained, but once this declaration was made, the murders stopped. Known as "Five Day Johnny" for his ability to crack the most puzzling cases in a short amount of time, Du Rose had around 300 special patrollers, 200 plainclothes detectives, and 100 extra uniformed officers, totaling up to 600 officers working on the case.

The investigation centered around searching for a location where the Stripper may have stored the bodies before dumping them where they were actually found. It was highly likely that the site would have to be close to a paint spraying plant. It was also assumed that Jack the Stripper may have been keeping the corpses in storage for even more sinister purposes, such as necrophilia.

The Suspects

It was a who's who of suspects when it came to someone as notorious as Jack the Stripper, and the suspects themselves came with their own notoriety. For instance, the involvement of a Welsh metal worker named Harold Jones was implied as recently as 2019. Jones' activities were reexamined by Professor David Wilson, a criminologist at Birmingham City University. Wilson's investigative team spent 15 months using offender and geographic profiling to unearth several similarities connecting Jones to the Hammersmith Nude Murders.

According to these findings, Jones had been living in West London at the time of the Stripper Murders and had a criminal past of his own. As a teen in 1921, Jones had violently murdered two young girls aged 15 and 11 but could not be sentenced to death for the offenses due to being a juvenile. He was released early from his life sentence twenty years later, following which he emerged in London. Wilson claims Jones had changed his name to Stevens after arriving in London and started working as a metal worker, which was the likely reason for the paint specks found on the victims' bodies. Unfortunately, Jones had never been suspected as the Stripper by the police, and he eventually died in Hammersmith on January 2, 1971. He was 64 years old.

Another suspect was a Scottish security guard named Mungo Ireland. John Du Rose referred to him as "Big John" in a BBC interview and he stated that Ireland was considered a suspect after Bridget O'Hara's murder because he had been working as a security guard at the Heron Trading Estate. This is where O'Hara's body was found, and the paint specks were traced back to. However, Ireland committed suicide right after this declaration, leaving a short note and inhaling carbon monoxide in a garage. It was also later uncovered that Ireland could not have been the murderer, as he was in Scotland when O'Hara was killed.

The most high profile of all suspects was Freddie Mills, a former British Light-Heavyweight Boxing Champion. This was postulated by a reformed ex-gangster Jimmy Tippett Jr., who was researching for his book on gang activity in London. Based on his findings, he concluded that Mills was "a sexually warped sadist who enjoyed inflicting pain" and had successfully hidden that side of himself thanks to his public image. Mills' popularity was one reason he could have been considered a suspect, as tabloid newspapers were more than ready to leap to conclusions just on the basis of hearsay. Nevertheless, the story took a morbid turn as Mills was found shot to death in 1965, possibly by suicide. Furthermore, the police had never seriously considered Mills as a suspect, but his death did put an abrupt end to the Hammersmith Nude Murders.

Another suspect was a former metropolitan police detective who held a grudge against his former colleagues. He faked burglaries in order to embarrass the police and was jailed for a year. But apart from living near the Heron Trading Estate, there was no solid evidence against him. Another interesting suspect was Kenneth Archibald, who admitted to killing Irene Lockwood right after Helen Barthelemy's body was discovered. But Archibald was acquitted shortly after he made this claim when it emerged that he had been drunk when he made the confession and had alibis for the other killings.

The Aftermath

Despite the rigorous amount of police work that went into investigating this case, Jack the Stripper was never found, nor was he identified. In just a year, he had spread a reign of terror among the citizens of London — particularly among the sex workers in the area. His brutal methods of strangulation and leaving his victims naked suggested Jack enjoyed the power he exerted over them. And yet, no one knows who the Stripper really was. Was he a former boxing champion? A security guard? Was he a disgruntled police officer or a child killer?

Much like the mystery behind his Victorian namesake from Whitechapel, it is most likely that no one will ever know the true identity of Jack the Stripper.

2

THE BLACK DOODLER

San Francisco, CA. 1974. A city teeming with radical enlightenment and welcoming people of all ethnicities and orientations. As it is popularly known, the Golden City became a haven for socially marginalized individuals such as lesbians, gays, bisexuals and transexuals, or LGBT, as well as outcasts and radicals. African-American and Latino-American populations also began to swell in greater numbers and turned San Francisco into a hub of cultural activity and innovation. And in the midst of it all, a sinister and sadistic individual began making his mark by killing at least five people, perhaps even more than 10. Not only did he kill them, but he also violated them sexually and even sketched them before committing the gruesome acts — thus earning himself the moniker of "The Black Doodler."

There is no official record or clue of who he is or where he came from. Though there has been no confirmation, the Black Doodler is believed to be alive and well, and even known to the several victims who managed to survive his attacks. Nevertheless, none of them will ever come forward to testify against him because most of the surviving victims themselves, while upstanding citizens with loving families, are also closeted homosexuals who wish to keep their sexual orientations a secret from their families and society. To this day, a reward of $100,000 is up for grabs for any information that may lead to his arrest. It is likely that this reward will remain unclaimed.

So, who was the Black Doodler? What deep-rooted psychological conditions fueled his desire to target homosexual men in San Francisco? And how has he remained at large for all this time?

The Golden City

The early '70s in the city of San Francisco saw a major cultural boom due to the blending of several multi-ethnic demographics at the time. There was a large influx of African-Americans, Japanese-Americans, and Chinese-Americans, as well as refugees from Vietnam and other Southeast Asian regions as the Vietnam war drew to a close in 1975. The city's Black population contributed greatly to the cultural upheaval, particularly with the rise of music genres such as jazz, jazz fusion, disco, and rock. Not only that, but San Francisco also became a hub for emerging musical acts in thrash metal, punk, and others, which made it the go-to place for music enthusiasts.

The Castro District

Located in Eureka Valley in San Francisco, the Castro district is one of the first gay communities in the United States. Throughout the 1970s, the Castro reinvented itself from a working-class neighborhood to a haven for gay, lesbian, and bisexual people all over the country. This was prompted by the arrival of thousands of gay servicemen from the United States military, who had participated in the Pacific theater during World War II. With San Francisco becoming an increasingly attractive option, previously settled residents began vacating the Castro, which left a great deal of real estate to be purchased by the gay community. The Summer of Love in 1967 saw a massive boom in not just the gay community, but also the hippie movement and the influx of drugs that came with it.

Bars, theaters, nightclubs, and even bathhouses with a predominantly gay audience were taking root, exploding into full-fledged tourist attractions for gays, lesbians, and bisexuals everywhere. There were businesses that catered to the needs of the LGBT community, and consumers and tourists could take in the sights and sounds of a freedom of sexuality that was lost to them in their own restricted locales. Shops, restaurants, and theaters, not to mention the periodic fairs that took place to bolster the area's economy made the Castro an economic powerhouse throughout the 1970s. It was the height of LGBT popularity before the AIDS pandemic of the 1980s.

The Emergence of The Doodler

It was in several of these newly established businesses — primarily the gay bars, restaurants, and nightclubs that had opened up in the Castro — where witnesses began spotting the man who would become the Black Doodler. One witness claimed that he had a conversation with the man before any of the killings started, wherein the Doodler contended that he was a commercial art student. Though he was visiting businesses frequented by many of the Castro's gay community as well as those coming in from the rest of the country, the Doodler did not appear to be there to engage in any sort of intimate relations. It has also been reported in surviving victim statements that the Doodler seemed confused about his sexual identity when he had spoken to them, and the police believed that he had mental difficulties related to sex. There are also matching statements by the victims wherein they were told by the Doodler, "All you guys are alike." This was his general understanding of all gay people, and certainly of all his victims.

It was surmised that the Doodler was a man of a quiet and serious disposition who appeared to have all the hallmarks of an upper-middle-class education. He is also perceived to have above-average intelligence, based on his methods and skill in remaining at large to this day.

The Victims

From January of 1974, the murders of several members of the gay community started to leave a trail of bodies in San Francisco that did not stop until September of 1975. Investigations initially led the police to believe that The Black Doodler was involved in killing 14 members of the gay community after physically and sexually assaulting them and attacking another three who survived. However, later investigations suggested the Doodler was responsible for just five or six of the murders, with no leads to any other killers.

Considering the pattern of his activities and those of his victims, it was surmised that the Black Doodler found all of his victims at the many gay businesses both he and they visited.

The Doodles

Based on the condition of the victims' bodies, it was concluded that the Black Doodler was known to sexually assault them and stab them violently to death. But, the most depraved of his actions was how he would make sketches of his victims — or, rather, cartoons and caricatures. This suggested to the police that he suffered from a psychiatric disorder apart from being unable to identify his sexuality. Later on in the investigation a psychiatrist made unofficial reports about treating the Doodler.

However, whether he was receiving any psychiatric treatment or not has never been officially confirmed. Furthermore, the investigations led to the belief that he was using these sketches to attract the attention of his victims.

The drawings played a crucial role in the way the Doodler operated, as he was sketching his victims in the establishments where he would find them. Naturally, the victims would undoubtedly be flattered, considering that it was an intimate kind of attention. Romanticism played an important part here, and it is evident that the victims were aroused by the attention they were receiving from someone who was drawing them at random. Thus, they would strike up a conversation, and when it was all said and done, the victims would follow the Doodler to take things up in a more private setting. Unbeknownst to them, this would be their most fatal mistake, as the Doodler would achieve his gratification by sexually assaulting and killing them brutally. The victims would never be seen alive again, and their bodies would be discovered in the neighboring waterfronts and parks.

The reason he became known as the Black Doodler was because of his dark skin tone. But it wasn't until November of 1975 that a composite drawing of the suspect was released, identifying him as Black and between the ages of 19 and 22 with a height between 5'10" and 6'0". He had a slim build and was spotted wearing a watch cap usually worn by those in the Navy. The sketches made by the Doodler himself were never released to the press or the public.

Gerald Earl Cavanaugh

Assigned the name John Doe #7, for the morning of January 27, 1974, Gerald Earl Cavanaugh was found dead at the edge of Ocean Beach in San Francisco. He was on his back and riddled with stab wounds. At the time, the body was examined at the scene. The coroner concluded that it showed signs of slight rigor mortis, but he was clothed and wearing a shirt, a jacket, pants, shoes, underwear, and socks. He had some money in his pocket and was wearing a watch. His left hand showed a defensive wound, which proved that Gerald had tried to fend off his attacker.

Born in Canada on March 2, 1923, Cavanaugh was a San Francisco resident who worked in a mattress factory. At 49 years old by the time of his murder, he was a Catholic and had never married. Gerald's hair was balding and he stood at 5'8", weighing in at 220 lbs. By all accounts, everything about him — including his life, his profession, and his personality — suggested that he was just a regular guy. But even after his death, it would be quite some time before Gerald Cavanaugh could be regarded as anything more than a simple, unassuming San Francisco resident who had been killed for reasons unknown. No one at the time could have guessed that the murder of Cavanaugh would only be the start of a brutal killing spree.

Joseph "Jae" Stevens

Months later, on June 25, 1974, the body of Joseph Stevens was discovered at Spreckels Lake, located in the Golden Gate Park. The body was found by an unidentified woman who recognized Stevens and called a mutual friend and avant-garde composer named Warner Jepson, who notified the police about the body. The coroner again conducted the investigation at the scene and concluded that Stevens' body was also stabbed at least three times, and his mouth and nose were full of blood.

Unlike Cavanaugh, who led a mostly average life, Joseph Stevens, nicknamed 'Jae,' was a popular stage performer until his murder. Born in Texas, Stevens made his mark as a well-known and entertaining female impersonator. His stunning impersonations of beautiful women enthralled the audiences at a popular San Francisco nightclub, though in his later years he was focusing more on performing gay comedy.

Witnesses claim that the 27-year-old Stevens was last seen at the Cabaret Club on Montgomery Street, located in the neighborhood of North Beach. According to the police, it is very likely Stevens and the killer left together. That was the last anyone would ever see of Joseph 'Jae' Stevens, and his entertaining persona would forever be lost to a violent murder.

The killing of Stevens would mark the second notch in the belt of the Black Doodler, even if the police hadn't realized it yet.

—

Klaus A. Christmann

Just a couple of weeks later on July 7, 1974, the body of Klaus A. Christmann was found where Lincoln Way ended at the beach. Upon preliminary examination, it was found that his throat had been slashed in three places and the rest of his body was covered in wounds from being stabbed at least 15 times. The investigating officer was Inspector David Toschi, who had also worked on the infamous 'Zodiac' murders, and he claimed that the murder was one of the most vicious stabbings he had ever seen. Christmann's body was found by Tauba Weiss, who was walking her dog Moondance at the time. She claimed that she ran after the dog once it started running towards the body. When she arrived at the spot where the dog had stopped, she saw a man lying down, unmoving. Weiss, herself a survivor of Auschwitz during the Holocaust and having lost her family to it, could tell easily that the man was dead, so she returned to her house and called the police.

As it turned out, Christmann was a German national employed by the Michelin tire company. He was 31 years old and was in the United States looking for a fresh start for himself. The police determined that the victim had homosexual characteristics, basing their assumptions on the fact that he was found wearing orange bikini briefs, a blue moonstone ring, and another brown cameo ring. He also wore a gold wedding band as well as a tan leather jacket, a white Italian Sela shirt, and black side-zipper ankle boots with brown Cuban heels. The police also revealed that he had a make-up tube in his pocket and that he was last seen alive at Bojangles, a popular gay dance nightclub.

Christmann's murder was instrumental in the police concluding that the earlier killings of Gerald Earl Cavanaugh and Joseph 'Jae' Stevens, along with this one, were connected. Nevertheless, it would be nearly a year later that the Black Doodler would strike again.

Frederick Elmer Capin

Around ten months later, a hiker caught sight of a body between Vicente and Ulloa Streets, hidden behind a sand dune. The victim was identified as Frederick Elmer Capin, a registered nurse who was also a medical corpsman in the Navy. The 32-year-old corpsman had received a commendation medal for saving the lives of four men during the Vietnam war. Because he was a registered nurse, Capin's fingerprint records were available to the state and he was easy to identify.

His body was found on May 12, 1975, wearing a blue corduroy jacket over a multi-colored Picasso shirt, both of which were soaked in his blood. There were also tracks found indicating that his body was dragged through the sand for at least 20 feet. The coroner reported he had been stabbed multiple times in his chest, the wounds mainly aimed at his heart and aorta. The coroner concluded that the stabbings were the primary cause of death.

Harald Gullberg

Just under a month later, the body of Harald Gullberg was found ten yards off a golf course trail at Lincoln Park. Gullberg had apparently been dead for nearly two weeks before his body was discovered on June 4, 1975 by another hiker. The police reported that his pants were unzipped and he had no undergarments beneath. His neck had been slashed violently and was subsequently considered to be the cause of death.

At 66 years of age, Harald Gullberg was the oldest victim of the Black Doodler. At the time, he was listed as unidentified John Doe #81 until it was discovered that he was a sailor. Originally from Sweden, he visited several harbors such as Boston, Puerto Vita, Cuba, Shanghai, Melbourne, San Luis Obispo, Yokohama, and Liverpool throughout the 1930s and 1940s, before finally settling in San Francisco in 1955.

Based on the pathologist's findings, Gullberg was suffering from portal cirrhosis, an end-stage liver disease that was killing him gradually.

The Survivors

With a body count of five gruesome murders, it was a miracle that three of his victims actually managed to survive the Black Doodler's deranged wrath. In May 1975, a European diplomat was stabbed six times in his own apartment. He admitted that he had invited the Doodler to his place after he had approached the diplomat in a restaurant. The diplomat confessed that the

Doodler had asked him for some cocaine, but denied any kind of sexual encounter. Considering the sensitive nature of his profession, the diplomat never revealed his identity to the press, no doubt fearing embarrassment, not to mention reprisals.

As reported by the San Francisco Sentinel, the other two survivors included a nationally popular entertainer and a well-known San Francisco figure. Nevertheless, both these survivors refused to be identified, nor did they cooperate any further with the investigation. The latter victim moved out of San Francisco shortly after the incident.

Speaking of the Sentinel, its reputation had also seemingly caught the eye of the Black Doodler. The previous owner of the publication, Charles Lee Morris, claimed he almost went to bed with a man who looked very much like the suspect from the police's composite sketch of the Doodler. However, Morris changed his mind at the last minute. The reason? A knife had fallen out of the man's coat. The story is difficult to substantiate, but it wouldn't be too far-fetched to believe that Morris' association with the Sentinel, as well as his own activism of gay rights put him in the Doodler's sights.

The Investigation

Once the police were able to identify the similar and gruesome nature between the murders of Cavanaugh, Stevens, and Christmann, they intensified their investigation into the matter by using several creative tactics. They surmised that the victims would no doubt be approached by the Doodler or vice versa, and then both of them would move to a more private setting, typically at the beach or Golden Gate Park. The setting of the late nights would ensure a reasonable amount of privacy for the pair to engage in any kind of sexual activity, which is where the Doodler would strike, or rather stab, violently and without mercy.

The police department's efforts to catch the killer appeared to be quite proactive; however, the larger old-guard of the department was rather un-empathetic to the plight of the gay community. On the one hand, creative police officers would use a type of entrapment to drive near a gay male matching the Doodler's description on the streets. Still, the largely Irish quarters within the department felt that the murders in the Castro were inevitable and that they "had it coming." The rate of homicide in the city had begun to rise from 112 in 1970 to 131 by 1976. This was also the time that the LBGT community saw sharp growth, yet the San Francisco Police Department had no gay police officers to speak of.

The Suspects

As time progressed, the police arrested many suspects and were even able to obtain a vehicle license plate number belonging to the main suspect. Eventually, the psychiatrist who had allegedly treated the Black Doodler came forward and was questioned by police. During this interview, the psychiatrist revealed that in a session, he had been informed by the suspect that he had committed the violent killings. Based on the San Francisco Sentinel's findings, it was also revealed that the suspect was actually heterosexual. No arrests were ever made due to a lack of evidence, even after the above admission.

The Witnesses

A significant obstacle in the police investigation was the stigma attached to being openly gay at the time. Nearly all the witnesses did not cooperate as they were reluctant to be revealed as homosexuals. Even though the investigating officers assured confidentiality, the witnesses and even some of the survivors were closeted at the time. They were unable to make such major revelations to their family and friends for fear of being ostracized by a society that had yet to welcome the gay community without prejudice.

The Aftermath

To date, there is no word on who exactly was the Black Doodler, nor does it appear likely that he will ever be found. The police have made no progress on the case, and it wouldn't be wrong to say that the nightlife and the residents of the Castro have probably seen the last of this killer.

3

THE MANCHESTER CANAL PUSHER

At the outset of the new millennium the Greater Manchester Area witnessed a surge in deaths with more than 60 bodies found in the waterways since 2004. These cases remain unsolved and these sites have since been dubbed "Manchester's Killer Canals."

But canals don't kill people. And while these waterways have become a popular site for disposing corpses, is there actually something more sinister afoot? What if these unsuspecting victims were pushed to their watery graves?

And thus was born the legend of the "Manchester Canal Pusher," believed to have killed anywhere from 61 to 86 people throughout the early 21st century. But while all these deaths have never been solved, the police have categorically and vehemently denied the involvement or even the existence of a so-called Pusher. Nevertheless, the area's waterways have gained a notorious reputation worldwide for the possibility of a serial killer lurking in the shadows, and reports of other killings in regions such as Yorkshire, Bristol, and London have been picking up steam. It could be just one, or it could be a whole gang, or it may even be copycats, warped minds picking off their victims at random.

So, what is it, then? An urban legend? A depraved maniac? A freak coincidence of several able-bodied and reasonably well-adjusted Manchester natives falling to their deaths in the water at night?

Who, or what, is the Manchester Canal Pusher?

The Canals

An extensive canal network runs through Manchester and connects the city's busiest neighborhoods, particularly the areas that are thriving at all hours. Since the development of Manchester as an industrial powerhouse during the 19th century, the canals themselves have seen quite a lot of growth, with about 10 miles of waterway running through central Manchester. Nevertheless, not much attention has been paid to make these canals pedestrian-friendly, particularly at night. Considering Manchester's skies are almost always gray, the frequent rainfall keeps the cobblestone paths along the canals slippery. This is further exacerbated by poor-quality fences along the canal and a surprisingly low amount of lighting at night.

Bars, pubs, and nightclubs run alongside the canal system that pierces through the heart of the city, and a considerable number of male patrons returning home full of alcohol are likely to venture out toward the canal. With a full bladder and few opportunities to find a public restroom, the dimly-lit canal provides a rather not-so-glamorous locale for the men to relieve themselves.

But does it also provide an opportunity for a sinister figure in the shadows to catch his victim unaware?

The Victims

The mysterious and shocking number of people falling to their deaths in the canals of Manchester have made people in the city feel completely unsafe and on edge whenever they pass by the city's waterways, even during the day. Social media has further driven the panic to a fever pitch, and the hashtag #ThePusher has been gaining traction online. Despite the unexplained number of dead bodies popping out of the canals, the police have yet to admit that foul play could be the cause of these deaths, let alone give credence to the urban myth of the canal pusher.

But the sheer number of bodies being found in the canals as well as the local rivers, the age group, the method of the disposal of the bodies, and the activities and lifestyles of the men who ended up in the canals have shown frightening patterns and statistics. Researchers looking into the mystery have stated that some of the men were doing perfectly normal things such as fetching groceries or meals on their way home, which makes it even stranger that their deaths could be categorized as suicides. Meanwhile, the families of the victims keep seeking out justice and raising awareness about what happened to their loved ones, about how their children were targeted and never seen alive again.

And according to some of their accounts, the events that led up to these deaths chilled them to the bone.

David Plunkett

On April 16, 2004, 21-year-old David Plunkett was on an organized trip with friends to a music event in Manchester. A student of Leeds Metropolitan University where he was studying event management, David ventured out with his friends from a bar in Leeds. He headed to the event in question, which was attended by more than 3,000 people. Apparently, David had quite a lot to drink, causing him to get rowdy and aggressive enough to be thrown out. One of the security personnel even claimed that Plunkett had vomited outside. His friends claimed that Plunkett was generally happy when he was drinking, and the aggressiveness he showed that night suggested that the drinks were spiked.

Two weeks later, his body was found in the Manchester Ship Canal on April 30, 2004, near the Imperial War Museum. According to the coroner, the cause of death was drowning due to being intoxicated by alcohol. The autopsy revealed that David's alcohol level was more than twice the prescribed driving limit. But his parents are wholly convinced that, in their son's last moments, David had been completely and utterly terrified by someone…

On the night of the event, his parents had been calling David after being informed by his friends that they had gotten separated. It was on the third attempt that he actually answered. However, they were puzzled that there was silence in the background while they were talking to him, despite the fact that he was supposed to be at a busy event. They had been talking for nearly ten minutes until 1:15am on April 17, 2004, as he kept telling his parents about the direction he was going. It was the last time they would ever hear the sound of his voice. And what they heard would leave them shattered beyond repair.

They could tell that it was their son on the other end. They could tell that he was frightened as he screamed on that call, using swear words they had never heard their son utter before. And worst of all, they could make out the sounds of their son being attacked before the call went dead. In that instant, they knew that David was fighting for his life. In one of the most frightening details to emerge, the police never did locate David's phone.

Even though his parents are entirely convinced that their son was murdered considering his "ghastly and unearthly" screams, the police have totally ruled out foul play and declared David's death as an accident. Nevertheless, his parents have denied that it could be anything but murder. Even former Detective Chief Superintendent Tony Blockley wondered if David had been lured or chased to the canal.

What was it that David saw that night? What was the reason behind his terrible screams?

Nathan Tomlinson

On December 17, 2010, 21-year-old Nathan Tomlinson — a resident of Stockport and a trainee sports teacher — went to a Christmas Party in Manchester. From reported accounts of the event, Tomlinson was seen exiting a bar where an unidentified woman slapped him across the face, though there is no credible eyewitness that can substantiate this. Eight weeks later, his body was found in the River Irwell near Meadow Road on February 10, 2011.

From the proximity of where his body was found to the nearest CCTV camera, the police were able to chart his route with the aid of the footage. After leaving the bar following the slapping incident, Tomlinson was seen jumping over a wall to get on Victoria Street. From there, he was spotted on Chapel Street in Salford until he was found walking near the River Irwell. On the night of his disappearance, Tomlinson had sent a text to his family that he was drinking shandy. But when his body was found, there was no phone on his person, nor a wallet, a coat, or even his passport

Though the police declared that his death was not suspicious, Tomlinson's mother maintains that there was foul play considering his belongings were not found with the body. Indeed, it is unlikely that anyone would have taken the belongings from a dead body to then throw the body into a river, so where did the belongings go? And how did Tomlinson end up in the river?

Chris Brahney

On June 29, 2012, 22-year-old Chris Brahney was attending a Stone Roses concert in Manchester. Ten days later, his body was found in the Manchester Ship Canal. The coroner could not conclusively state what had caused Brahney to end up dead like this in the water, as there was little DNA evidence to be gathered thanks to the body being submerged for so long. The only thing the coroner could conclusively state was that there were traces of the drug ecstasy in his body. Though the coroner confirmed that Brahney might have drowned due to being under the influence of drugs, she recorded an open verdict since she could not determine the actual cause of death. But Brahney's parents and friends will never be at peace without uncovering the truth.

After the concert ended at Heaton Park, Brahney was separated from the rest of his friends and was never heard from again. A barman by trade and a resident of Timperley, where he lived with his parents, it was initially assumed that he might have stayed the night with his friends. But once he did not return home by Sunday, his parents were in a panic, he was not answering his phone and his friends had no idea of his whereabouts. His friends and family prompted the police to conduct a large-scale manhunt around the area in order to find his whereabouts, but unfortunately, he would not be found alive.

On July 9, 2012, Brahney's body was pulled out from the canal near Media City. Once it was identified, the police were able to use the CCTV camera footage to chart out the path of his final journey. As he was seen moving through the city, Brahney was spotted getting off a tram at Victoria Station where he retrieved a bag containing shoes. Apparently, he had left them there in order to change into them after the concert. Once he had left the station, he made his way to St. Mary's Parsonage through the city center, moving onto a walkway along the riverside. The walkway only had a four-foot railing. A resident from an overlooking flat stated that he saw someone with Brahney's description on the walkway that night. He was supposedly just sitting there.

The autopsy of Brahney's body revealed traces of alcohol and MDMA; however, these were not ruled the cause of death. Furthermore, Brahney also had a fractured cheekbone and cuts on his face. Since there were no bruises with the injuries, these appeared to have happened after he had died. Even the senior investigating officer cited that the CCTV footage did not show any evidence that Brahney was too drunk while charting his path to the walkways, nor did he appear to be injured. It was also revealed that Brahney suffered from mild anxiety a couple of years prior, but his mental state at the time of his death was positive and definitely not suicidal.

So, if Chris Brahney, a perfectly sound and reasonable individual, was in no state to take his own life, what pushed him into the canal that night? What, or whom?

Souvik Pal

On New Year's Eve of 2013, 19-year-old design student Souvik Pal disappeared from a dance night at Warehouse Project in Trafford Park. Apparently, he was caught jumping a line for the toilets and had been ejected from the premises by the door staff. His body was found three weeks later, about 50 yards from the park in the Bridgewater Canal. Upon investigation through the CCTV cameras in the area, it was discovered that Pal had been seen with a mystery man right before his death. This has made his father, Santanu Pal, firmly believe that his son's death was caused by none other than the Manchester Canal Pusher.

The mystery is further compounded when other CCTV footage shows someone climbing a fence near the water to get back into the club. The police believe this is Souvik Pal, trying to get back to his friends in the club. Police found it odd, though, as this would have required Pal to swim through the water in order to get there. Nevertheless, there were no witnesses who could back this claim, as the other figure in the CCTV footage could not be identified.

After his arrival from India to attend university, Pal had started taking drugs and drinking alcohol and was quite popular among his friends. His enthusiasm and zest for life made him seek out new avenues for enjoying himself, which was why he was so driven to attend the party on New Year's Eve that night. He had apparently taken ecstasy with alcohol before he went into the club. When he did not return to his flat the following morning, his flatmate reported him missing. The autopsy on Pal's body revealed no injuries and certified the cause of death as drowning.

With such an upbeat personality, Pal had a large circle of friends who loved and adored him so much that they gave testimony in court regarding his death. It is highly unlikely that Souvik Pal would have knowingly taken his own life that night. Which begs the question, who was that figure seen in the CCTV cameras with him, and what does he know about Pal's death?

The Survivor

In April 2018, a 34-year-old cyclist was returning home from work at around 10 o'clock at night near Bridgewater Canal when he was attacked by a figure in the shadows that swung to knock him down into the water. The cyclist, who wishes to keep his identity undisclosed, tried to pull himself out of the water only to be pushed and kicked right back in by his attacker. Though he managed to get out and survive, the attacker was long gone. Aware of the reputation of the killer canals of Manchester, the cyclist was convinced that this was the work of the Manchester Canal Pusher.

The cyclist, a father of two, pointed out that the lighting was virtually non-existent along that path, making it very easy for all sorts of foul play to take place there. He claimed he could have drowned as his legs were caught up in the bike. Aside from the person who pushed him in, the path was completely isolated, and no one could have come to his aid.

He was disappointed to learn, however, that the police were treating this as an assault rather than attempted murder. Authorities also made no affirmation of the claim that this could be the work of the same serial killer who had been pushing his victims in the canal since 2004. Nevertheless, the cyclist was able to give a description of his attacker as a man between the ages of 20 and 40, of average height, and wearing a black jacket. The lack of illumination at night, not to mention the ferocity of the attack, made it difficult for the victim to get a really good look at the attacker.

The Legend of the Canal Pusher

With such a high body count emerging out of the watery graves of the Manchester Canal, speculation is rife that it is indeed the work of a sinister individual. The press agrees and adds more fuel to the fire of the theory that a sadistic serial killer continues to terrorize the city's residents. With very little evidence and a lack of admission by the law enforcement agencies, residents of Manchester are wary about being too close to the canals, and the myth of the Pusher continues to permanently entrench itself among the masses.

The Motive

A likely reason for the police to consider all the deaths taking place in the canals as unrelated is the lack of any obvious motive to link the victims. None of the people pulled out of the canals from 2004 to date were connected in any way, and were mostly either drunk and partying through the night or just making their way back home. As is a consistent pattern with serial killers in general, most kills come out of an unhealthy obsession or a lack of empathy toward their victims, and also might involve revenge, passion, or even a single personality trait among the victims that made them stand out. Though many serial killers seek sexual gratification from their kills, this does not seem to be the case for the Manchester Canal Pusher. Can it be assumed then that the Pusher has a vendetta against people walking or cycling along the canals? Or does he have the need to see people drown? Or perhaps his attacks are completely at random so the Pusher can stay one step ahead of authorities.

The Method

Another hallmark of the Pusher's legend is the murder weapon: the canals themselves. Using the water as the means of death and final resting place, the Pusher solves the problems of not just killing and dumping the victims, but also uses the water to wash away any traces of DNA or forensic evidence that could provide any leads to the police. The absence of such evidence might be the reason why the authorities have never considered this to be any more than unfortunate and completely unlinked accidents.

Manchester also happens to be one of the most vibrant cities in the country with a bustling nightlife, and this is proven by the extensive network of CCTV cameras that cover the busiest corners and streets of the area. For the Pusher to operate so successfully and without being detected proves the killer has sound knowledge of the streets, the corners, the restaurants, and the clubs that surround the canals — as well as the coverage of the CCTV cameras around the area. Not to mention the black spots where it would be all too easy for him to commit his sinister crimes. Up until now, the police have relied on CCTV footage to trace the last steps of most of the victims, but there was no conclusive camera footage of how they ended up in the canals.

So, if the police continue to deny the existence of a cold and sadistic serial killer pushing his victims into the canals of Manchester, just what is the cause of so many able-minded individuals with no link whatsoever to find themselves condemned to a cold grave without any explanation? Were all of them too inebriated to know what they were doing? Was the protective barrier around the canals woefully inadequate to keep people from falling in?

One thing is for sure: the 'myth' of the Manchester Canal Pusher, as the police call it, continues to grow stronger with each day, and the bodies from the canals never seem to stop coming. And while the police continue to maintain that there is no Pusher at all, the aggrieved families of the poor victims know in their heart of hearts that their children met with something that led them to their doom. Something, or someone.

4

THE CHICAGO STRANGLER

C hicago, Illinois: a city that is no stranger to violent crime of all kinds from the beginning of the 20th century. The famous visages of gangsters, such as Al Capone and Dion O'Bannion brandishing Tommy guns while wearing fine pinstripe suits, immortalized the Windy City as one of the most dangerous places in the world to live. This reputation from the 20th century has carried over to the next, as more than 75 women since 2001 have been found brutally murdered in locations across Chicago. Whether in abandoned buildings, parking garages, garbage cans, dark alleyways, or vacant lots, women of all ages, races, and professions have been discovered dead — strangled or asphyxiated to death — with a large portion of them being sex workers.

While some of the cases have been solved, to this day there are 51 victims families seeking justice for the strangulation of a loved one. All evidence points to a sinister figure that has become both feared and reviled for his continuous brutality: the Chicago Strangler.

The sheer amount of violent crime taking place in Chicago coupled with the fact that most of the women killed by the Strangler were from marginalized communities has seemingly had a negative impact on the investigation. It appears that bringing a killer to justice is simply less of a priority for law enforcement because of who is being killed.

Authorities claim otherwise, but the distinct nature of the crimes being replicated repeatedly does not give credence to the theory that these were all isolated and unrelated incidents. The way multiple bodies have appeared almost one after the other without a clear trace or evidence suggests a great deal of foresight, planning, and calculation on the part of the Strangler, if indeed it is just one person.

The Victims

What makes the Chicago Strangler even more frightening is the fact that no credible witnesses have come forward in the unsolved cases. Since he has been operating across the city with absolute impunity, his body count continues to increase, with no telling how many more have yet to be discovered. Violent crime continues to plague Chicago, with the second deadliest day in the city's history taking place in 2020. The citizens fell in shock after reports of 18 killings in just 24 hours on May 31. It makes one wonder just how much the Strangler could have benefited from this chaos.

The pattern of the kills is also quite telling of the Strangler's designs, as the women to face his wrath have been of various ages, races, and ethnicities. These victims often had their own struggles with all sorts of vices such as drugs, prostitution, and abuse, not to mention run-ins with the police on some occasions. Such circumstances left these women vulnerable to the most vicious of predators, and their untimely and unfortunate deaths all across the city from the south side to the west side. These neighborhoods have long suffered at the hands of drugs and violence, and too many of the women here would inevitably get caught in the trap of the Chicago Strangler.

It seemed as though the violent streak of the Strangler knew no bounds, as his victims were anywhere from 18 to 58 years of age, including one who was a grandmother and another even a great-grandmother. Racial overtones could not be overlooked as several of these victims were African-American women. Still, while that may be a critical factor in itself, a vast majority of the women strangled to death were either actively or formerly involved in prostitution or were caught up in cycles of drug addiction that had crippled their lives. Nevertheless, some were trying to rehabilitate themselves and get their lives back on track, a few of them hoping to finish school and become nurses or waitresses to reclaim what they had lost. This makes the Strangler's actions all the more devastating.

The Stranglings

As many as 47 of the victims of the Chicago Strangler were involved in the sex trade at one time or another. In a profession where women offer their bodies for the right price, the risk of suffering at the hands of a frustrated client is alarmingly high. Not to mention that most clients seeking sex have certain fetishes which provide them not just sexual gratification but also a kind of gratification that allows them to feel powerful, superior, and entirely in control of their 'merchandise.' Sex workers have reported being choked by clients, typically unwanted but some would actually allow themselves to be choked if the money offered outweighed the consequences. In the case of the 47 victims, we may never know if the Strangler even gave them a choice.

Furthermore, the Strangler took his time with each of his victims, as he made them feel completely and utterly helpless. From the autopsies conducted on the victims, there were clear signs of physical assault and rape, not to mention bruises and intense head injuries, and even a broken nose in one case. Some bodies discovered had their faces trapped in plastic bags.

And if that wasn't enough, the Strangler took it a step further by setting two dead bodies on fire in November 2007 after violently strangling them and putting them in trash bins like garbage. One of the victims was eight months pregnant.

Margaret Gomez

In January 2006, the body of 22-year-old Margaret Gomez was found in a salvage yard hidden underneath a tractor. All she had on was a T-shirt, a bra, and socks, and she had been stabbed in the neck and shot in the back of the head. Gomez also had a piece of rope tied around her neck.

The road that led Gomez to her eventual fate was riddled with hardships. Once a promising young woman who had been on the cheer squad and enthusiastic about art, she suffered from low self-esteem and constantly sought approval from her peers. Her mother kept a strict household for her daughters, including Margaret. This is what could have led Gomez to become rebellious as she became addicted to drugs thanks to a boyfriend she doted on. No longer the obedient child, Margaret Gomez would go missing for days on end until she would return home a complete mess and out of her senses.

Her family did all they could to get her back on the straight and narrow, and Gomez seemed to be coming out of her drug-filled haze by earning her GED followed by receiving First Communion in the Catholic church. But the crippling addiction would be her undoing, as she eventually left home in pursuit of a high for the very last time.

Perhaps it could be easy to believe that it was the drugs that strangled the life out of her, but the rope around her neck is clear proof that it was the Chicago Strangler.

Theresa Bunn

The most heinous of the Chicago Strangler's killings wouldn't be discovered by the police until November 2007. On the fateful Monday night of November 12, 2007, the police found the body of a woman in her 20s who had been strangled to death. She had also been stripped bare and put into a dumpster, which was then set ablaze with a flame accelerant. The police had to resort to dental record verification as the body had been burned beyond recognition, but it did not escape their notice that she was eight months pregnant. The woman was identified as Theresa Bunn, a 21-year-old Black woman who had graduated from high school three years before her brutal murder. She had gone missing earlier in the evening when she had headed out to a mall but never returned.

Her family described her as radiant and full of life, but she had been arrested once over the matter of her confronting the man responsible for her pregnancy. There is no telling what deep, dark secret led to Bunn being targeted by the Chicago Strangler; and to be put to flames in such a fashion that it took the authorities three days to positively identify the body.

Hazel Lewis

Theresa Bunn may have been the first victim to be burned, but she was definitely not the last. Just over 24 hours after Bunn's incinerated corpse was found near Washington Park in Chicago's south side, the body of 52-year-old Hazel Lewis was discovered only a few blocks away. The second body had also been set on fire after being stuffed inside a trash bin and doused with an accelerant, becoming unrecognizable before the firefighters arrived at the scene.

A mother of three daughters and even a great-grandmother, Lewis was also Black, just like Theresa Bunn, and had suffered a nearly identical fate, pointing to the involvement of the Chicago Strangler. The autopsy revealed that Lewis had been strangled just like Bunn a few days earlier, and her body had been torched not too far away from Bunn's. Lewis was also 52, which went to show the Strangler wasn't deterred by age when it came to choosing his victims. The grotesque manner in which both Lewis and Bunn had been set fire to revealed his callous disregard for the women, treating them as nothing more than garbage.

Neither case has been solved to this day.

Amy Martinez

The Strangler struck again with full force six years later. On a Sunday night in May 2013, the body of Amy Martinez was discovered by firefighters in the northwest of Chicago. Like Bunn and Lewis in 2007, Martinez had also been strangled and stuffed into a dumpster before being set on fire. Martinez, however, was Hispanic rather than Black, but that was as far as any differences would go between the three women who had suffered a fate so cruel. No clue has emerged for any of these victims, and no arrests have been made so far.

Catherine Saterfield-Buchanan

The Strangler struck again. On June 23, 2017, Catherine Saterfield-Buchanan, another Black woman, was found on the west side. Her body was partially naked when residents in the area came upon her. She had been strangled to death and suffered defensive wounds over her body, mainly on her face, as she appeared to have been severely beaten. But the Strangler stayed faithful to his moniker, and the autopsy proved that she had died due to strangulation.

At 58 years of age, Saterfield-Buchanan was the oldest of the known victims and had apparently seen many years of trauma and abuse in her life. Before her death, she had found herself at a shelter for women experiencing poverty, homelessness, and escaping prostitution. It was revealed that Catherine had a history of learning disabilities and had been arrested once for solicitation.

Her case, much like the others, remains unsolved, and the Strangler remains at large.

The Investigation

So far, the police have closed 25 of the cases after arresting 13 men, but that still leaves a staggering 67% of the cases unsolved. The police had been actively collecting DNA evidence from the crime scenes, which was entered into the Combined DNA Index System (CODIS), but so far, none of the DNA collected from the strangulation victims could be matched. Furthermore, no link has been found between the DNA evidence collected from all the strangulations, which leaves the likelihood of this being the work of the same serial killer up in the air. Even the FBI has joined in the pursuit of solving the remaining 51 cases.

Investigations conducted by both the police and independent crime watchdogs revealed a glaring pattern in all of the unsolved cases over the last 20 years. The victims were all women, with over 70% of them Black. The victims were found mostly or partially naked, with their clothing ripped by force in order to brutalize the nature of the assaults on them before their deaths. Speaking of assaults, the victims had been on the receiving end of violence, not just at the time of death, but also throughout their lives.

A history of prostitution was also recorded in several of the victims, which gives credence to the assumption that the victims may have known their killer in some capacity as a client. If they didn't have any history of prostitution, then it is very likely that they had been sexually assaulted by force. Other similarities included drug addictions, indicating most of the victims were leading a very unhealthy and "high-risk" lifestyle.

The victims were murdered mainly by strangulation using all sorts of items such as belts, ropes, garrotes, and to make it even more personal, the bras that the women were wearing. There were also plastic bags found on some of the victims' faces, showing that the killer also resorted to asphyxiating his victims. Furthermore, the bodies themselves were almost always found outdoors or in secluded areas such as alleyways, abandoned properties, vacant lots, and hidden spots in parks. This suggests the killer had no qualms in leaving the bodies exposed and actually went out of his way to make a grotesque display of his victims.

Investigations have revealed that the locations where the bodies were discovered followed an unusual but obvious route that trailed from north to south. This could mean that the killer was hunting the women along these paths as they were known to be secluded, ensuring less possibility of being spotted. Also worth noting is the fact that these areas were not likely to be heavily policed, considering the already rampant street crime and gang violence in the more central parts of Chicago. Because the victims of the strangulations were women from marginalized and "at-risk" backgrounds, the reports of their deaths took less precedence in the news against the headlines of gun or gang violence, and the like. Thus proving that there is not only prejudice in the way violence against women is investigated, but also reported.

The Involvement of a Serial Killer

Because of the lack of any tangible links between the victims as well as the DNA evidence collected at the crime scenes, the police maintain that this does not appear to be the work of a single serial killer or an organized ring of serial killers using the same modus operandi. Nevertheless, the manner with which the women were selected, assaulted, and then strangled using similar implements such as bras and articles of clothing makes it appear that the Strangler wanted his kills to be as up close and personal as possible. This has been the main reason why the public at large believes this to be the work of the same serial killer, and it is a fate that terrifies them to no end.

The Public Outcry

Naturally, the public living in the surrounding areas, especially the neighbors and loved ones of the victims themselves, are horrified at the thought of a serial killer still being at large. If we are to believe the police's claims that it is not likely that this is the work of a serial killer, that means there are potentially 51 murderers out there still living and breathing in the same city. Because of the obvious correlation between the victims and prostitution, public advocates have called for better protection for sex workers who frequently fall prey to abusers, violence, and eventually murder. Not to mention there should be rigorous prosecution against known offenders of sexual violence against sex workers, as well as better CCTV coverage of areas that are hotspots for prostitution.

Speaking of CCTV coverage, in the areas and secluded locations where the bodies were discovered, residents have called for serious steps to be taken to improve visibility. Abandoned places such as buildings, garages, lots, and alleyways lack adequate lighting, let alone CCTV cameras, and this creates the perfect avenue for a killer to strike.

The authorities may claim that the remaining unsolved cases are not connected, but the public isn't buying it. For now it seems the Chicago Strangler has his sights set on the Windy City and his hands firmly around its throat.

5

THE BRABANT KILLERS

In the province of Brabant in Belgium, a gang of men terrorized the area with their reign of vicious and violent crime. Known locally only as "the Giant," "The Killer," and "the Old Man," the Mad Killers of Belgium struck in the early 1980s, killing 28 people and injuring a further 40, as well as robbing several businesses and even a textile factory. Although technically classified more as "spree killers" than serial killers, their story is so fascinating that it must be included here. They do, in fact, remain at large to this day, and a reward of €250,000 is still up for grabs for any information that would lead to their arrest.

As they would later come to be known, the Brabant Killers have left scathing wounds among the residents of the province that remain even after Brabant was split into three territories in 1995. Their reign of terror was further amplified by the sheer audacity and temperamental nature of the three as they cared little for the amount of violence that they dished out, bordering or even crossing the limits of sanity — earning them the moniker of Mad or Crazy Brabant Killers. But as their sinister plans and schemes started coming to light, investigators discovered the three were far, far more ruthless than anyone could have ever imagined.

The Robberies

The Brabant Killers struck with full force in 1982 when they started a string of armed robberies around the small towns and larger cities in the Brabant Province. Armed with a single 12-gauge shotgun, the trio barged into a store in Dinant to commit their first robbery on March 13, 1982. They moved on to grand theft auto as they stole two vehicles at gunpoint a few months later. Up until August that year, the Gang of Brabant — as they were then called — continued to rob grocery stores, restaurants, and other odd businesses. But at that point they hadn't even caused any injuries, let alone started killing. But that was all about to change. On August 14, 1982, they forced a shootout against the police in the middle of robbing a grocery store. Two police officers were injured as a result of the encounter.

If their earlier crimes gave no indication of their brutality, the events of September 30, 1982, would lead them to the point of no return. The gang made their most daring robbery attempt yet as they stormed an armaments store in Brussels in broad daylight. Showing not just their audacity but their level of insanity as well. While holding the store's occupants, including customers and employees, at gunpoint on the floor, the Gang of Brabant started relieving the store of all its high-end weaponry, including handguns, shotguns, and semiautomatic rifles. Eventually, the police arrived, and another shootout ensued. This time, one police officer was shot dead while two others were seriously injured. Thus the gang had officially graduated to be known as the Brabant Killers.

The Murders

On December 23, 1982, the body of Jose Vanden Eynde was found inside the Beersel Inn. A retired taxi driver, Vanden Eynde, was the caretaker of the Beersel Inn when it was attacked by the Brabant Killers in what appeared as a robbery. However, the condition of Vanden Eynde's corpse suggested that he had been tortured mercilessly before being killed. This could also be the reason for the robbery itself, as the Brabant Killers must have targeted the inn specifically to get to Vanden Eynde. But why?

It soon emerged that the victim was a vocal supporter of former Spanish dictator General Francisco Franco. This caused even more confusion in the police investigation as the motivation for the murder was completely unlike the modus operandi of the

Brabant Killers. Since Vanden Eynde's assassination, as it were, did not match the usual style of the trio, the police were wary of linking all their crimes.

Before the sun would rise on January 9, 1983, the Brabant Killers murdered a cab driver named Angelou Constantin and stuffed his body in the trunk of his own taxi. When the police checked the cab, they found a cigarette butt with the corpse, which tested positive for DNA. Nevertheless, no matches were ever found to unearth the identity of any of the killers, but this gruesome act cemented their reputation for being utterly callous.

The following month, however, the Brabant Killers committed grand theft auto and several armed robberies of grocery stores, but surprisingly did not leave any bodies in their wake. This kept on mystifying the police and the public regarding the gang's mercurial tendencies as their exploits varied from damaging to fatal. This flip-flop approach was used again on March 3, 1983, when the Brabant Killers stormed a grocery store and killed the manager, even after he had opened the safe for the attackers. The gang also kept firing warning shots that could have seriously injured the other customers in the store as well as the bystanders outside. So, even though their activities would vary from no fatalities to direct murders, the Brabant Killers clearly did not care at all for any innocent life around them.

A few months later, the gang stole around $20,000 from a grocery store in Houdeng-Goegnies on May 7, 1983, followed by a robbery at an automobile workshop. Though there were no fatalities in those encounters, the Brabant Killers would again change course by breaking into a textile factory on the night of September 10, 1983. They killed the night watchman and seriously wounded his wife, while also threatening the eyewitnesses who were there. The factory had only recently started manufacturing bulletproof vests, seven of which the gang made off with.

A week after, the Brabant Killers struck at a supermarket to rob it when a couple pulled into the parking lot in their car. The gang took the couple hostage but also came under fire as the police responded to the scene. The couple was killed along with a police officer, while another officer was seriously wounded. The Brabant killers used the couple's car as the getaway vehicle, even battering through police roadblocks with it.

Toward the end of an especially violent year, the Brabant Killers ran roughshod and unabated as they killed a restaurant owner in Ohain while robbing his establishment on October 2, 1983, followed by killing a grocery store manager in Beersel and wounding three customers five days later. They capped off their reign of terror in 1983 on December 1, when they attacked a jewelry store that was connected to the owner's residence in a small town called Anderlues. The gang forced their way into the store and killed the owner's wife. The owner himself tried to shoot at the killers, but he was also killed. However, the daughter of the store owners survived unharmed, which led to the police getting visual descriptions of the killers.

In almost all of the robberies of several businesses throughout the region that year, the Brabant Killers obtained little to no monetary gains. However, their trail of blood left many devastated families in its wake. The public was in fear for their lives, but they were also left in suspense. Inexplicably, the Brabant Killers made absolutely no known moves in the year 1984. The entire province of Brabant was on edge, and the police continued looking for them; however, they seemed to have vanished off the face of the earth. But it was only a momentary reprieve. Just as everyone started to breathe easy again, the year 1985 saw the Brabant Killers return with a vengeance.

They started back with a supermarket in Braine l'Alleud on September 27, 1985, where they killed a customer and took a child hostage before making their way in. They entered and made their escape from the market, but not before injuring another customer in the store and killing the driver of a white van outside. The child was also wounded but left alive. Others were not so lucky.

And still others would not be. Just 30 minutes later, the Brabant Killers struck at a grocery store in Overijse, where their barbarity knew no bounds. They shot and killed a hostage in the store and also shot the cars moving outside. But the most heinous of all their acts in Overijse was the murder of a child who was playing outside with two others. Overijse mourned the death of five of its residents that day, all because of the savage and insane acts of the Brabant Killers. The public outcry against these violent and unforgivable crimes intensified and could not be ignored any longer by the corridors of power.

But the worst was yet to come. In the small town of Aalst, the Brabant Killers forced their way into a supermarket with pump-action shotguns, shooting and killing victims outside in the parking lot with reckless abandon before even getting inside the store. Once inside they didn't stop, as they murdered an entire family, including a nine-year-old girl. Only her brother survived. According to eyewitnesses, the Brabant Killers laughed maniacally as they killed the hostages inside and shot at the store clerks. It would be their most gruesome and brutal outing yet, as The Brabant Killers claimed eight lives on November 9, 1985. And yet, surprisingly, it would also be their last.

The Descriptions

Thanks to eyewitness accounts from the survivors who were up close and personal to the gang in those attacks, the police were able to discover more details about the band of three. Without any positive identification, the killers were given nicknames based on their descriptions, such as "the Giant," mainly for being quite tall at 6'4", but also for being the apparent leader of the gang in all of the robberies and assaults. He was slim and had a small birthmark on his neck that resembled a wine stain, based on the testimonial of one witness.

The second member was aptly named "the Killer," as he was single-handedly responsible for 22 of the 28 killings committed by the gang. Witnesses also claim it was "the Killer" who would laugh maniacally as he gunned down his victims. He had a dark complexion and spoke with a fluent and exotic French accent. He was also tall and slim like "the Giant," but there couldn't be two giants in the gang.

Finally, the third was known as "the Old Man." Like "the Giant" and "the Killer," the third member of the gang appeared to be no less than 50 years of age. He had a quiet disposition as well as a short stature compared to the other two tall and flamboyant members of the gang. The witnesses also claimed that "the Old Man's" main role in all the attacks and robberies was that of the getaway driver, though he would also be ready to brandish a shotgun of his own.

The Method

Based on the eyewitness testimony as well as the accounts from the surviving police officers who were caught in the shootouts against them, the Brabant Killers were described as utterly callous with complete disregard for the safety of the general public. The way they would brandish their weapons as soon as they would step out of their vehicle and start shooting at hapless bystanders was akin to bandits terrorizing towns in the Old

West. The way the gang would shoot first and make demands later made anyone caught in their crosshairs frightened for their lives, if they were in fact able to survive the encounter.

But underneath the more glaringly obvious veneer of ruthless and mad criminals hell-bent on terrorizing the populace, an even more sinister and shocking truth was realized by the police. Based on evidence and testimonials, the Brabant Killers were thorough professionals in all of their attacks and assaults on stores and factories. They hit with precision and brute force and were more than capable of using a shotgun. They formed a straightforward pattern of attack and escape, which could even suggest that they had researched all the sites that came in their line of fire. Furthermore, they proved themselves to be completely superior to law enforcement as the Brabant Killers were able to not just escape, but injure and even kill several police officers.

Therefore the possibility that the Brabant Killers were actually trained combat specialists, even former soldiers or militia members, cannot be ruled out. Worse still, they could have even been actively part of the military when they committed their heinous crimes, if the incredible manner in which they disappeared after committing each one is anything to go by.

The Investigation

Even after nearly four decades, the police have not come anywhere close to unearthing the true identities of the Brabant

Killers. Furthermore, the public outcry against this lack of success led many of the public to believe that the investigation had been corrupted. Rumors that there may be inside connections between the police and the gang were rife. Because not only did the precision and professionalism suggest that the Brabant Killers could be former police officers, but that could also explain why their escape from every crime scene was so successful.

The businesses and victims chosen by the gang also do not appear to be random, but carefully selected targets which suggests that something even more sinister was behind their actions. In all of the attacks, the accumulated amount stolen from the cash registers of the various businesses does not seem to outweigh the amount of trouble that the gang undertook, particularly with all the armament they had utilized to commit those felonies and murders. And in some cases, such as the restaurants, the only items stolen were bottles of champagne, coffee, and other delicacies. This lends credence to the theory that the robberies and invasions of the business were a facade for targeted assassinations, though no substantial evidence to prove this theory has been found.

The Evidence

Even as recently as 2020, the authorities have been collecting DNA profiles of members of the public to have a large enough database in order to match the evidence they have been able to obtain. Specifically, two crucial pieces of evidence found at the crime scenes contained some DNA traces. First, there was the cigarette butt found in the trunk of the taxicab, along with the murdered corpse of the driver in January 1983. The second trace of DNA was found on a bulletproof vest that had been cut up and worn by one of the gang. The vest was fished out of a river in 1986.

The Conspiracy

Speculation that the activities of the Brabant Killers were far more sinister than just the robberies and murders on the surface gained fever pitch in 2014, when a man named Michel Libert was questioned by the police. This was of significance, as Libert was a former lieutenant of a right-wing terror organization called the Westland New Post (WNP). This organization was notorious for launching attacks against businesses, shops, and cafés throughout the country that were owned by the immigrant and Arab populations in Belgium. Organizations such as the WNP have publicly gone on record stating that these attacks were carried out at the behest of NATO to curb Communism in Europe, and the exploits of the Brabant Killers formed a significant part of this operation. Though Libert was detained by the police for questioning, he was released shortly after without being charged.

The Suspects

In 2017, a monumental event rocked the investigation, as a man from Aalst approached the police, claiming to be the brother of one of the Brabant Killers. This man claimed that his brother, Christiaan Bonkoffsky, was in actuality the man referred to as "the Giant," a serving member of an elite Belgian police unit in the gendarmerie until he was fired in 1981. According to the man, Bonkoffsky had died in 2015 and confessed to being one of the Brabant Killers on his deathbed.

The reason Bonkoffsky was fired, as alleged by his brother, was the result of an accidental discharge of his weapon while on duty. This created resentment within Bonkoffsky, which caused him to lash out as part of the Brabant Killers. Though this would appear to have been a landmark development in the case, the DNA collected from Bonkoffsky did not match that found at the crime scenes.

There were also other notable suspects identified primarily for their association with not just the police force, but with certain criminal elements as well. This list includes two former police officers named Madani Bouhouche and Robert Beijer, who were responsible for selling firearms to extremist groups within the country. Then, there was a former prison director named Jean Bultot who, along with a well-known criminal named Philippe De Staercke, had connections with a gang of jewel thieves that were notorious for conducting violent and blatant heists that smacked of those by the Brabant Killers. Another major suspect was Patrick Haemers, a renowned gangster, convicted rapist, and drug abuser who was part of the group that had abducted the former Belgian Prime Minister Paul

Vanden Boeynants for ransom in 1989. However, Haemers committed suicide in prison in 1993.

The Legacy

For the better part of the early 1980s, The Brabant Killers terrorized and terrified unsuspecting residents of the region of Brabant with their audacious, vicious, precise, and, above all else, gruesome attacks that destroyed families and ripped apart the sanctity of life. The fact that the gang showed no remorse or even a twinge of humanity as they brutally executed 28 people with smiles on their faces reeks of complete barbarism and brutality. Not to mention that none of their crimes were fueled by a sufficient motive, which made their overwhelming attacks completely senseless and ultimately devastating.

No one was spared, not even children. And considering that the statute of limitations for their crimes has all but run out, it looks as though the people of Brabant will never get justice for the precious lives they lost.

6

THE ATLANTA RIPPER

As the ashes of the American Civil War were blown away with the winds of change in the early 20th century, the American South was bracing itself for a major social upheaval. None of this was more evident than in Atlanta, Georgia, known for being the last stand of the Confederacy, as tensions continued to mount over racial equality after slavery had been abolished. But in the midst of such turmoil, an even more sinister and shocking threat lurked in the shadows to prey upon helpless Black women.

Believed to have killed around 15 to 21 women, the Atlanta Ripper rocked the uneasy peace in the city. His brutal actions of killing most of his victims by crushing their skulls and almost decapitating them fueled the rage among already marginalized Black communities. Not only did they have to deal with this violent murderer, but also the sheer lack of any interest among the mostly white law enforcement agencies tasked to bring this monster to justice.

The Gateway to the New South

Having rebuilt itself in the 40 years since it was burned down by Major General William T. Sherman, Atlanta regained its lost abilities to conduct trade with other towns and cities using the railroads by 1911. Though endeavoring to be more racially tolerant on the outside, the divide among the white and Black populations was still quite great. All menial jobs with long hours and the more impoverished and neglected localities for homes were relegated to the Black community. This was primarily due to segregation, which ensured that Black families would not be allowed to live in "white" neighborhoods.

Violence had also reared its ugly head, as around 40 Black men were killed in a rampage by white people in 1906. The reasons for this stemmed from reports of Black men attacking some white women; however, it only highlighted the continuous deep-rooted fear and bigotry among white people to find any opportunity for a reaction. Because of segregation, boundaries had been established for Black people with specific places in the city deemed for whites only, including "white" restaurants, parks, bars, and so on. Black people were not even allowed to drink water from "white" fountains, nor could they bury their dead in "white" cemeteries.

Nevertheless, the city did offer some glimmers of hope as businesses owned by Black proprietors began to take root in the city, as well as schools of higher learning such as Atlanta University, Atlanta Baptist, and Morris Brown College.

But in an environment still full of mistrust and hatred, the Atlanta Ripper thrived as he

executed his murderous designs with impunity and with little fear of law enforcement agencies. Sure enough, despite the initially high body count, neither the police nor the press gave the murders of innocent Black women much attention.

The Victims

The Atlanta Ripper literally carved out his reputation, not just by terrorizing the city of Atlanta, but also by his method of killing. The use of blunt objects such as rocks and bricks and other heavy metallic objects such as train car pins became his hallmark, as he bludgeoned his victims to death. But what made his murders even more shocking and brutal were the near decapitations of the women. He would pick several places on the victim's heads to carve through their throats, slashing them from ear to ear and even mutilating the rest of their bodies. On many occasions, he even cut their shoes off — and in almost all cases, he dragged the bodies out into the streets for the public to discover.

All the victims of the Ripper were Black or biracial women, who were easy for him to approach considering the strict segregation laws at the time. Furthermore, the violence and brutality that he exhibited against the women suggested that he had a deep-rooted hatred of them, possibly even fear of some kind.

The Coming of the Black Butcher

Considered to be the very first victim of the Atlanta Ripper, Maggie Brook was found near the railroad tracks on October 3, 1910. The 23-year-old cook had her skull fractured.

Four months later, Rosa Trice was found with the left side of her skull completely crushed, similar to Brook. But the 35-year-old Trice suffered an even more gruesome fate on January 22, 1911, as her jaw and throat had been cut open with the intention of decapitating her. Once she had been killed, her body was dragged from her house out into the middle of the street, to be found in public view. It was suspected that her husband was responsible, but there was no evidence found against him. Nevertheless, the authorities had yet to make a connection between the cases.

But the Ripper was just getting started. His next victim was another cook named Mary Walker, whose body was found on the morning of May 28, 1911, outside her home. Known as "Belle," Walker had been left with her throat cut open and she was dragged out into the street. The police had no clues regarding the party responsible.

A similar grisly fate befell Addie Watts, whose skull was crushed with something large, such as a brick or a train coupling pin. Her body was found in some shrubbery near the railway. Much like Trice and Walker before her, her skull had been stabbed and her throat slit wide. She was dragged to where she was found on June 16, 1911, after her

murder.

By now, the local press had begun to report on the incidents, as a headline declared a "black butcher" terrorizing Black women. While this was brief coverage that didn't stir many emotions, it did link the crimes to the infamous Whitechapel murders of 1888. This may have captured the imagination of locals that Atlanta had its very own Ripper, but the police still maintained that there was no serial killer responsible.

The Summer of 1911

The summer of 1911 continued to heat up as the body of Lizzie Watkins was found a little before noon on June 24, 1911, in some bushes. The same method of execution was used, as her throat had been viciously slashed and her body had been dragged outside. Watkins' murder finally brought the reports of the crimes to the front pages of the local press, where the similar methods of killing were given more coverage than ever before. Furthermore, the connection with Jack the Ripper from Whitechapel grew even further as it was speculated that the Atlanta Ripper also had some anatomical knowledge. But another newspaper reported incorrectly that the woman had been killed due to a drug and alcohol overdose, highlighting the ongoing apathy in most quarters toward the killings.

The drama grew to a fever pitch on July 1, 1911, when the body of 40-year-old Lena Sharpe was discovered. This proved to be a significant development as, for the first time, there was an eyewitness account. Even so, the press still managed to stir confusion in the minds of the public with two contrasting accounts of the killing.

One reported that Lena's 20-year-old daughter Emma Lou went seeking out her mother, who had gone to the market but had not returned. Her fear grew even more when she discovered that Lena had not even made it to the market and intensified, because their neighbor was Addie Watts, who had been killed only recently. But on her way home, Emma Lou ran into a tall Black man wearing a wide-brimmed black hat. Sensing danger, Emma Lou attempted to walk past him when he said, "Don't worry. I never hurt girls like you." Then, shockingly, Emma Lou screamed as she felt a stab in her back, and the man ran off, laughing. Once her neighbors brought her home, Emma Lou was distraught to find that her mother was still missing. Ultimately, it was only a little while before her mother's body was found, with her throat slashed open and her head lying in a pool of her own blood.

Another newspaper described both Lena and Emma Lou walking to the market together when they were attacked by a Black man. As he emerged from his hiding place, he beat Lena's head in with a brick and then proceeded to attack Emma Lou, which is when he stabbed her. Emma Lou managed to escape from the scene but fell unconscious to the blood loss. When she did regain consciousness, she saw the same Black man hovering over her with a bloody knife in his hand, after he had slashed Lena's throat to shreds. It was only the sound of oncoming footsteps that prompted the attacker to run away. In this version of events, however, the attacker did not say a single word.

At last, the police detectives decided not just to link the man who had attacked both Emma Lou and Lena Sharpe, but also to connect him with the murders of the previous victims.

The Headlines and Arrests

The brutalized corpse of Sadie Holley was discovered by a workman on the morning of July 11, 1911, when he followed a trail of blood on his route to work. Holley, a worker at a local laundry, was found with her skull bashed in and her throat slashed from ear to ear. It was also discovered that her shoes had been cut off from her feet, and a bloody rock was next to her body. The Rock is what was apparently used to bludgeon her to death. There were even some tracks in the dirt, which marked the path her killer took to escape the scene after dragging her body there.

Holley's murder gained a much larger audience than all the others, as there was a crowd of nearly 500 onlookers at the scene. Her death also made it to the front page of the most prominent newspapers in an article highlighting the previous murders that had been largely ignored.

Another major development occurred just under 24 hours later when the police arrested Henry Huff, the first suspect linked to these murderers. A 27-year-old laborer, Huff was not only the last person that witnesses placed with Holley before her death, but his trousers had blood stains as well as dirt up to the knees. His arms had also been scratched up.

As if one arrest wasn't enough, the police also held Todd Henderson after claims from a witness that the 35-year-old was with Holley in a drug store close to the scene of the crime on the night she was killed. The drama intensified when Emma Lou Sharpe, the girl who had been attacked a few weeks earlier, was asked to identify Henderson as the man who killed her mother. When she heard his voice, she shrank back in fright and informed reporters that he was the man. Even Henderson didn't do himself any favors as he stated on the record that "if I were the Ripper, I would have begun on my wife."

Nevertheless, the evidence against both Huff and Henderson was circumstantial at best, and the police were still nowhere near to capturing the real killer, as was proven the following month.

The Spree Continues

Were either Huff or Henderson the Atlanta Ripper? The murdered corpse of 20-year-old Mary Ann Duncan begged to differ. She was found between the railroad tracks with her throat slashed and her shoes cut off from her feet on August 31, 1911.

A few months later, Eva Florence was murdered at the hands of the Atlanta Ripper in a field on October 22, 1911. This time, only her head had been crushed, her throat remained intact. Nevertheless, her body had been dragged out to where it was found, and it was also reported that people heard the sound of a firearm shortly before she was killed.

The Ripper seemingly struck again in under a month as Minnie Wise was found with her head bludgeoned and her throat slashed. Not only that, her shoes were missing, and her right index finger had been severed from her hand. This was a new characteristic in the Ripper's M.O. Furthermore, Wise was also dragged to a location that was near to where two previous victims were found.

In the early hours of November 21, 1911, the body of Mary Putnam was found in a ditch with not just her throat slashed and her skull broken, but also her chest ripped apart with her heart pulled out and left next to her corpse. As the ditch was surrounded by dirt, the police discovered footprints for which they used a bloodhound to track. The dog managed to trace the scent for about 200 yards but no farther.

The Lull After 1912

The New Year would start off on a bloody note as the body of Pearl Williams was found near a vacant lot on January 19, 1912. A cook by trade, like some of the others, Williams was found with her throat slashed. It appeared as though she was murdered on her way home from work in the evening.

But the Ripper began to slow down, as it was a couple of months before the next victim was found. This was Mary Kates, who was found with her throat slashed and her body ripped open on April 8, 1912. It was reported that a surgical instrument had been used for the mutilations on her body, which lends further credence to the theory that the killer could have some knowledge of human anatomy.

Nearly a year later, the Ripper struck again. The body of Laura Smith, a servant, was discovered with a slashed throat in March 1913. Then, a year later, 17-year-old Zeulla Crowell was found in the river after being missing for three weeks on February 11, 1914. Though the location where she was found differed from the usual open streets that the Ripper would leave his victims in, it was obviously his handiwork as Crowell's skull was broken in three places.

The Investigation

Due to the shocking nature of the crimes and the grotesque manner in which the bodies were displayed, the crowds of onlookers at the scenes made the police's job more difficult. It was likely that this was the Ripper's intention, as this would disturb vital evidence such as footprints and so on. Despite increasing police patrols, they seemed to prove no match for the Ripper who expertly moved around the town, particularly the areas of the railroad where most of the bodies were found. This has also led to the speculation that the Ripper was not even a resident of the city, and that he would only arrive into town by train on the weekend. It may have even been possible that the Ripper was employed by the railway company, which gave him unfettered access to the surrounding areas.

Another disadvantage the police suffered was the lack of cooperation from members of the Black community. Despite questioning several Black onlookers from the scene, and relatives or loved ones of the victims, they were rarely given any tangible leads that could help the authorities locate the killer. Worse still, it was also believed that some in the Black community were aware of the killer's identity or whereabouts, but refrained from divulging it. This could either have been because of the fear of their own lives from the Ripper's wrath, or a belief that the authorities would not take their statements seriously because of racial prejudice.

The Racial Divide

The likeliest reason for the Atlanta Ripper's prolific violence was his opportunity to kill without raising an eyebrow. This was proven by the local press, which relegated such murders to back pages of the newspapers. Even if attention was given, the fact that it was Black women being murdered garnered little sympathy from the city's influential elite. A vicious killer targeting helpless women did not concern the movers and shakers in the city's administration simply because the victims were not white.

When the press reported the murder of Lena Sharpe and the subsequent attack on her daughter Emma Lou, the newspaper articles were less concerned that women were being killed with their throats slashed open and more concerned about the murders of the domestic help. Other reasons the press gave for the lack of interest was a general assumption among the white populace that Black people got rowdy and out of control on weekends when their liquor consumption increased. By that point, fights and attacks under the influence of alcohol among the community were commonplace.

By all eyewitness testimony, especially by some survivors such as Emma Lou Sharpe, it was a safe conclusion that the Atlanta Ripper was indeed a Black man. This can be further attributed to the inconspicuousness of a white man being found in a Black neighborhood, as any presence of a Caucasian male near a Black woman could have invited scandal, if not outrage. This would hold especially true for any white men found near the scene of the crime, as racial tensions in the era of segregation were already quite high. But a Black man, a person who would not look out of place in a Black neighborhood, would not have such difficulties moving from house to house and murdering the hapless women at their own door before dragging them out to be found on the streets.

Thus the Atlanta Ripper carried out his dastardly designs on an unsuspecting populace with a fury that stirred outrage and disgust among the Black community. And the fact that it was one of their own made them shudder at what lay deep inside the hearts of men.

7

THE MONSTER OF FLORENCE - AKA: THE ZODIAC?

L ove kills, literally — and it has in the case of Florence, Italy, where a ruthless and methodical menace plagued the hilly countryside, striking unsuspecting men and women who were only there to have a good time. Between 1968 and 1985, the "Mostro di Firenze," as he is locally called, killed 16 people as he targeted couples under dark, moonless nights when they would arrive in the countryside to get intimate. His cunningness and patience in going after a couple the minute they started to undress for intimacy was one thing, but the sheer brutality with which he treated the corpses of the dead women in his murders is what has given him the above moniker, translated literally as "the Monster of Florence."

The Florentine Countryside

The historic city of Florence is itself quite a tourist attraction, thanks to its exquisite architecture as well as art galleries boasting fabulous works from the Renaissance period, not to mention delectable cuisine. As if that weren't enough, the surrounding countryside is renowned all across the globe for its majestic hillsides as well as scenic cypress trees and olive groves, making it an idyllic attraction for tourists from all over. Even before the agriturismo laws of 1985, which allowed local farms to host a large number of tourists, the place had its own share of visitors all year round.

The splendid sunflower and poppy fields create a rich and charming atmosphere that fuels notions of romance among the young couples visiting, or choosing this spot just for their own craving of intimacy and peace — a perfect setting for a perfect crime of passion. But, in this case, several crimes.

The Slayings

One would think that driving out to an isolated area in the countryside would allow loving couples the opportunity to get intimate, if they could manage to do so inside their vehicles. It was these very hotspots young lovers used to frequent that provided the Monster of Florence the opportunity to carry out his kills and thrills. Firstly, the timing of the encounters had to be carefully thought-out, as he would pick dark nights with low moonlight to venture out for couples — which, ironically, could have been the motivation of the couples, as well.

Furthermore, the nights he chose were usually weekends or holidays, which meant the couples he would attack would not be immediately missed at places such as work and home. This suggested a carefully considered plan of attack, not something that was done on an impulse. The Monster would also vary his locations after each attack. He ventured out into other parts of the suburbs around Florence, taking his time and discovering more hotspots for couples to be alone for the last time.

And that was precisely what he did, as the Monster hid in secluded spots for extended periods, waiting until the car was parked and was rocking sufficiently for things to get underway. Knowing this would be the only time the couple's minds were totally focused on each other, the Monster would pounce upon them during the act of sex and shoot both the man and woman dead with a gun before conducting the ritual of mutilating the woman's body. This brutal and violent act was also well-thought-out and precise, as he used a scuba knife to remove the women's remaining clothes and butcher their sexual organs.

However, the Monster apparently never gratified himself sexually at the crime scenes in any way, as there was no evidence of rape or even necrophilia on the corpses. All that concerned him, it seemed, was to satiate his bloodlust.

The Gun of the Mostro

Among the Monster's signature calling cards, the most mysterious has always been the Beretta .22 caliber pistol used in all of the crimes he committed. The weapon was unique due to its singular use of Winchester series-H bullets embossed with the letter H. These bullets were determined to have come from the same stock and all found to be manufactured before the year 1968. Another unique quirk of this particular weapon used in the murders is a small mark left upon the shell casings because of the gun's defective firing pin, which proved conclusively that the gun and the murderer involved in all the killings were one and the same. But up until now, there has been no trace of the gun, which has baffled the police and other investigators. And yet, this weapon and its bullets, with all their unique quirks and characteristics, are what makes the mystery of the Monster of Florence an absolutely tantalizing one.

Barbara Locci and Antonio Lo Bianco

On August 21, 1968, Barbara Locci and Antonio Lo Bianco parked their car in the woods on the outskirts of Florence. They appeared to be having an extramarital affair, as they were both married to other people. Unbeknownst to them, a sinister figure pounced upon their romantic revels and shot them both dead. But, in a cruel twist, the killer didn't realize that Locci's six-year-old son Natalino was sleeping in the back seat. Thus it is believed that the killer carried him over his shoulders to a house nearby. The boy remembers that the man was singing; however, this account would frequently change, considering that Natalino was quite young at the time of the murders.

Barbara Locci, 31, was married to a much older man named Stefano Mele, but was also the lover to a group of three Sardinian brothers working around Florence. They were not just laborers but also petty criminals and were able to take advantage of Mele's mental disadvantages to be Locci's sexual partners. Since this was the first time such a crime had taken place, the police concluded that Mele had caught on to his wife's adulterous relationships and had caught her and the 29-year-old Lo Bianco red-handed. Mele himself also seemed to provide a confession, but would then retract it and put the blame on the Sardinian brothers. At one point he even admitted that he had dropped the murder weapon somewhere but could not recall exactly where, and the police gave him a paraffin glove test to prove he had used a gun recently.

The case was basically an open-and-shut crime of passion and revenge, and Mele had the perfect motive to kill his wife. He was convicted, but not punished too harshly, considering his mental infirmity and old age. Meanwhile, the murder weapon would never be found — but it would be used once again. The Beretta .22 caliber was used in the murders of Locci and Lo Bianco, but they wouldn't be its last victims.

Pasquale Gentilcore and Stefania Pettini

It would be six years after the murders of Locci and Lo Bianco that the countryside of Florence would see more blood spilled. On the night of September 15, 1974, 19-year-old Pasquale Gentilcore and 18-year-old Stefania Pettini were getting cozy in their car when they were shot dead by an unsuspecting intruder. The gun used was a Beretta .22 caliber, just like in the murders six years prior. And this time, the killer would become the 'Mostro.' Once he had killed the couple, he pulled Stefania Pettini's body out of the car and proceeded to stab her sexual organs around 100 times with a knife. He also violated her corpse with a grapevine before fleeing the scene. The police could unearth no leads in the investigation, and the suburbs of Florence would remain at peace for a time.

Giovanni Foggi and Carmela De Nuccio

About seven years later, the Monster would strike again. On June 6, 1981, Giovanni Foggi and Carmela De Nuccio were in their car fulfilling their passions when the Monster of Florence shot them both dead. This time, he also cut open 30-year-old Foggi's throat. Then, just like he had done with Stefania Pettini all those years ago, he mutilated 21-year-old De Nuccio's corpse and cut out her vagina. It was never found and led investigators to believe that the Mostro collected it as a trophy.

Stefano Baldi and Susanna Cambi

There would be no reprieve for the lovers in Florence, as the Monster was just getting started. After only four months, he unleashed his wrath once more by killing 26-year-old Stefano Baldi and 24-year-old Susanna Cambi on the night of October 23, 1981. Once he had shot both Baldi and Cambi, he mutilated the woman with his knife and also removed her vagina just like he had with Carmella De Nuccio. One would have thought that the Mostro would have disappeared again after killing in June, but it seemed as though he was making up for lost time.

Paolo Mainardi and Antonella Migliorini

About eight months later, Paolo Mainardi and Antonella Migliorini were murdered in their vehicle on June 19, 1982. This time, however, the Monster was prevented from satiating his bloodlust fully. Even after getting shot, the 24-year-old Paolo Mainardi was able to back up his car into a crowded street, which startled the passersby present at the time. Afraid of being found out, the Monster fled the scene, and therefore the body of Antonella Migliorini was spared a fate far more gruesome than death. Though the 20-year-old Migliorini was killed instantly from the gunshot, Mainardi survived long enough to get the car away from the killer, but breathed his last at the hospital.

Wilhelm Friedrich Horst Meyer and Jens Uwe Rusch

Over a year later, after the unfulfilled ritual of the Monster of Florence, another disappointment of sorts came his way on September 9, 1983. That night, he tracked and shot down two victims, both 24 years old, but was undoubtedly shocked to discover they were both men. German tourists Wilhelm Friedrich Horst Meyer and Jens Uwe Rusch were caught off-guard in their vehicle, and it was apparent the Monster had mistaken Rusch as a woman because of his long blonde hair. Much like the last time, there was no mutilation of the corpses, considering that his pattern was to only mutilate women.

Claudio Stefanicci and Pia Gilda Rontini

The Mostro kept quiet for about another year until July 29, 1984, when he claimed the lives of 21-year-old Claudio Stefanicci and 18-year-old Pia Gilda Rontini. The police found the couple's bodies and discovered the woman's left breast had been cut off along with her vagina and her entire pubic area. During the investigation, it emerged that Pia Gilda Rontini had been hassled by a man on the night of the murder who treated her quite unpleasantly.

Jean Michel Kraveichvili and Nadine Mauriot

The Monster would strike one last time at the beginning of September 1985, when he ambushed 25-year-old Jean Michel Kraveichvili and 36-year-old Nadine Mauriot in their tent in the woodlands. Both victims were French tourists and were asleep in their tent when the Mostro attacked, shooting Mauriot to death and wounding Kraveichvili, an amateur sprinting champion who managed to flee to quite a distance. This prompted the Monster to chase after him in order to finish him off.

As for Nadine Mauriot, her body was butchered severely as he cut up her left breast and vagina. To add insult to injury, the state prosecutor received a note from the Mostro containing Mauriot's nipple, taunting the authorities. Amidst such insane confidence, the Monster of Florence fell silent after racking up his 15th and 16th kills.

The Investigation

It has been over 50 years since the Monster of Florence first struck, and even with all of the efforts put into the investigation, the killer's identity remains a mystery. The Italian authorities enlisted the talents of experts in the field such as investigators, criminologists, psychologists, and sociologists, not just locally but also internationally, as the matter was out of the local police's area of expertise. In the beginning, the police were unable to comprehend the concept of a serial killer, and in the case of Barbara Locci and Antonio Lo Bianco, they had sent the woman's husband to jail under the assumption that the husband was getting even for being cuckolded by his wife. Crimes like these weren't typical of the local countryside. So when a villain like the Mostro emerged into their reality, it felt as though the entire situation was a Hollywood script with a killer straight out of a slasher flick.

The Profile

Even the FBI's Behavioral Science Unit jumped on the scene after a request from the Italian Carabinieri. However, the official veracity of this request has always been in doubt. From their expertise in such cases, the unit crafted a profile that has never been issued to the local press. The profile painted the Monster of Florence as a man who hated women and made it his mission to drive that point home with the way that he brutally mutilated their sexual organs. The fact that he never committed any kind of sexual assault himself on the victims could signify his own sexual inability or impotence. The ritual of destroying and even taking sexual organs for himself as trophies showed he had some kind of mental need to use those trophies to relive the thrill of the kill, which may also explain why he took extended breaks between several of his murders.

The Mostro was believed to be a careful planner, as he would obviously scout his victims beforehand in order to carry out his attacks. He also had an ample supply of Winchester H-series bullets that he used for all of his kills, and the fact that they came from the same stock suggested that he had gathered those bullets for a singular and twisted purpose.

Despite appearing to have an insane level of confidence to execute his assaults, in reality, he wanted to keep control at his end and would be depleted of confidence when things did not go according to plan. This was especially true in the cases of Paolo Mainardi and Jean Michel Kraveichvili, who actually attempted a reasonable escape, which threw a wrench into the Monster's plans.

The Convictions

Stefano Mele was the first man to be convicted right after the murder of his wife and lover, based on his flip-flop confession that did not hold up to the evidence available—especially considering that similar and ghastlier killings would take place six years later using the same murder weapon. Another man named Pietro Pacciani was accused of being the Monster of Florence. A man known for his short temper, Pacciani was responsible for stabbing a man to death and raping his girlfriend while the corpse grew cold next to them in 1951. Furthermore, his house was thoroughly searched, where the police not only found some German household products that may have belonged to the victims, but also a buried .22 caliber bullet.

However, neither of these men were the Monster of Florence. While Mele was in prison at the time of the other murders, Pacciani was, in fact, convicted in 1994 for seven of the double murders. But in his appeal in 1996, a public prosecutor declared the evidence against Pacciani was "circumstantial and unsound," and he was acquitted at the age of 71.

The Zodiac Connection

The Monster of Florence was unlike anything the country had ever seen. The brutality with which he picked off his victims and mutilated the women's genitalia had the public frightened. He was committing vile and despicable acts that no one could wrap their heads around. The sheer number of relentless stab wounds on the victims themselves made even the police's stomachs turn. The audacity of his note to the authorities taunting and mocking their ineffectual efforts to find him as well as sending a piece of a victim's breast showed that the killer held nothing sacred. To them, this was impossible. But thousands of miles away across the Atlantic Ocean and on a completely different coast, there was another killer operating on a similar level in northern California, United States: the Zodiac Killer.

Like the Monster, the Zodiac Killer would shoot the male victims before the female ones. Like the Monster, the Zodiac Killer went after couples looking for sexual intimacy on dark, moonless nights, particularly on the weekends or holidays. Like the Monster, the Zodiac Killer also used a .22 caliber handgun, among others, and also carried a knife, which they both used to stab their victims repeatedly. Like the Monster, the Zodiac also taunted the authorities with a cruel note. This has led to speculation that both the Monster of Florence and the Zodiac Killer were one and the same.

There were differences, however, as the Zodiac Killer was not known to have mutilated the sexual organs of the women as the Monster did. Also, while both the Mostro and the Zodiac Killer started operating around 1968, all of the murders committed in the U.S. took place after Florence witnessed the first killings in August 1968. This could suggest that if the killers were the same person, he might have started committing his crimes in the

United States before claiming his subsequent kills in Florence in 1974. Furthermore, while there were no mutilations of genitalia in the U.S., the Zodiac Killer had written in one of his letters that he would, in fact, commit such mutilations.

Whether or not they were the same individual, the fact remains that the last victims of the Zodiac Killer breathed their last in 1969. But the hills and countryside of Florence would see more blood spilled well toward the turn of the century.

8

THE BUTCHER OF MONS

There are killers and stranglers, as well as slayers and rippers. There are even monsters.

And then, there are the butchers — murderers so vile, so sadistic, so animalistic, that they don't leave an inch of their victims untouched. The savagery with which they treat the bodies could make anyone doubt how such people exist in the world, and how they live and move about society without getting a second glance. They exist like wolves in sheep's clothing. Ready to pounce.

Which brings us to the Butcher of Mons, a moniker not given lightly considering his reputation and the way he treated his victims. Known to have operated in the Belgian city of Mons, close to its border with France, the Butcher of Mons killed five people in a single year from 1996 to 1997 and lived true to his name by chopping up their bodies into separate parts. Then, once he had committed his heinous crimes, the Butcher left their remains near the roads around the city in garbage bags, reducing their lives to nothing but pieces of meat in the literal sense.

Despite two suspects who were caught for totally separate murders, the mystery of the Butcher of Mons continues to haunt the minds of Belgians to this day, as no one truly believes this sadistic maniac has ever been caught, or ever will be.

The City of Mons

A once heavily fortified city dating back to the 12th century, Mons is a quintessential European town featuring elegant brick-laden architecture and several exquisite churches and chapels. The city showcases a number of memorials for the epic WWI battle that took place on its grounds and is also a hub of commercial activity and university education. It shared the honor of being the European Capital of Culture in 2015.

But underneath the old-world rustic charm that most European cities possess to attract tourists from far and wide, the truth hiding within Mons' history is a vicious and horrifying one that people would soon rather forget. And yet it hangs over the city like a specter ready to rear its ugly head, for it has never truly been vanquished.

The Victims

No one has ever witnessed how the Butcher of Mons operated in and around the town, or at least no one has lived to tell the tale. It is only by piecing together the evidence, the clues, and the remains of the victims themselves that police have been able to establish a pattern of the Butcher's activities. Based on the profile of most of the victims, it appears as if the Butcher targeted women who were down on their luck, mostly living alone having no social contact with any family or friends, perhaps even ostracized from their relatives for one reason or another. Some of them also had children but were separated from them due to divorce or domestic issues, and some even frequented secluded spots such as railway stations and train tracks. At least two of them had a history of engaging in heavy drinking and meaningless sex among the patrons of the bars they visited.

Whether or not they had suicidal intentions can only be determined by their state of mind, which appeared to be at an all-time low. This state of despair is what provided the Butcher of Mons with the perfect opportunity as he picked off each of his unsuspecting victims one by one over the course of two years. He would methodically and, of course, brutally rip away their dignity and their lives by slaughtering them and chopping their bodies into pieces. It is yet to be known if the victims were actually alive when he ripped them apart.

The Discoveries

Aside from individual body parts that were found scattered in various secluded areas of Mons, the first discoveries of body parts in garbage bags were made in March 1997 by Officer Olivier Motte along the Rue Emile Vandervelde in the village of Cuesmes. Mons and Cuesmes are a very short distance from each other, and the report of the garbage bags stuffed with body parts shocked the small towns. Upon further analysis, the investigators were able to determine that the severed body parts belonged to three victims, all of them women of varying ages.

But that would not be all, as the following day, Mons itself would be the site of more garbage bags discovered around the city. Body parts, including a woman's torso, were in those bags, and it appeared that they had all been removed surgically. Based on the limbs, the investigators concluded that at least one of the women was murdered as far back as 1995, and another killed only a few days prior to being found in March 1997. More limbs and body parts were found in the Haine River, which led the police to believe that this was indeed the work of a serial killer. As is the case with most serial killers, it was a matter of when, not if, the Butcher would strike again.

Carmelina Russo

Forty-two-year-old Carmelina Russo had been dealing with depression caused by some personal tragedy in her life, which prompted her to visit secluded places such as the railway stations of Mons on a regular basis. On one such night of January 4, 1996, Russo left her house and never returned. No one would see her again until January 21, 1996, when her pelvis was discovered at the border close to the Nord region of France.

The fact that Russo could have been dealing with depression right before her death forms a pattern for the rest of the victims. It appears that the Butcher of Mons was exclusively targeting women who were vulnerable and seemed to be cut-off from society, at least mentally.

Martine Bohn

On July 21, 1996, Martine Bohn was reported as missing. A 43-year-old transexual prostitute from France, Bohn shuttled back and forth between France and Belgium, where she plied her trade at disreputable and sleazy underground bars in both countries. Bohn liked nothing more than to while away her time drinking alcohol and engaging in meaningless sex, which could explain why she never managed to keep contact with any of her family members. Furthermore, she also didn't have many friends outside of her contacts in the sex trade, which could explain why the Butcher targeted her.

The partial remains of her body — mostly her torso — were found floating in the Haine River by fishermen. Upon piecing together as much of her remains as possible, the police were able to identify the body as Bohn's. They also made the startling discovery that her breasts had been sliced off, which was concluded as the killer's way of highlighting the fact that Bohn was transsexual.

Bohn's murder, and the condition of her remains, suggested the Butcher of Mons was indeed not just motivated to kill simply for the sadistic pleasure of cleaving meat, but was also fueled by lust for sexual gratification of some sort, a common hallmark for serial killers.

Jacqueline Leclercq

On January 23, 1997, 33-year-old Jacqueline Leclercq went missing. Much like Carmelina Russo, who went missing a year before, Leclercq had been separated from her husband and had lost custody of her three children. This had caused her great pain and mental anguish, as such heartbreaking situations do, and therefore Leclercq was known to have frequently visited the train stations in Mons similar to how Russo had done.

Months later, Leclercq's arms and legs were found by an officer right under Rue de Emile Vandervelde in Cuesmes on March 22, 1997. However, the limbs were discovered in garbage bags with no clue as to the whereabouts of the rest of her body. The police feared the worst. Leclercq was the first of three victims whose remains would be found at Rue de Emile Vandervelde in separate garbage bags — at least eight of them — by Officer Olivier Motte.

Eight bags, three victims. The Butcher of Mons was just getting started.

Nathalie Godart

In March 1997, Nathalie Godart disappeared after being last seen at one of the many bars in downtown Mons. The 21-year-old was a mother to a child who had been taken into public care because of Godart's ongoing domestic issues. She was living in a rundown bedsit in Mons and became a regular visitor to bars where she was popular among the men for being quite promiscuous in the number of lovers she took. She never prostituted herself for money, however, and the staff at the establishments made that clear to the police.

Depressed over the situation with her domestic life and her child, Godart continued to drown her miseries in alcohol and sex before her disappearance on any one of those nights. Her body, or the remains of it, was also found in the Haine River, just like Martine Bohn's was in the previous year. At 21 years of age, Godart was the youngest such woman to be found dismembered and in pieces in Mons. But she certainly would not be the last.

Begonia Valencia

In the summer of 1997, Begonia Valencia vanished after leaving her house in Frameries. Half a year later, her bones and skull were found in an orchard between Bethleem and Hyon. It took the police a year to officially identify them as those of the 37-year-old woman who used to take the bus every evening within Mons. This emerged from an interview with one of her neighbors, who spoke out ten years after the incident. The neighbor mentioned that Valencia would take the bus punctually every evening and talked about a person who would drop a wreath of flowers over a river in town, supposedly in remembrance of Valencia. Though the police have not been able to substantiate the claim, this person could be the one responsible for Valencia's murder, the Butcher of Mons himself.

The Investigation

It never takes long for psychiatric analysts within the police department to provide theories about how the mind of a serial killer works, and this proved to be the case for the Butcher of Mons, as well. By all accounts, the Butcher was a puzzling breed, with the manner of his kills and disposal of the bodies varying from vicious and beastly hackings to more surgically precise and meticulous, bordering toward obsessive perfection. Nevertheless, it was very likely that the Butcher was surgically and medically trained and, much to everyone's horror might even be an active part of the medical fraternity. This appeared as a likely possibility considering that the victims mostly disappeared on weekends, which indicated that the killer remained busy with a day job throughout the week.

Aside from the actual slayings, the Butcher was theorized to have a sadistic sense of humor based on the locations where he would leave the garbage bags containing the body parts. The names of these locations had different meanings locally, such as the Haine River meaning 'hate' and the Trouille River, meaning 'jitters.' Other sites such as Rue de Depot and Chemin de l'Inquietude meant 'Dump Street' and 'the Path of Worry,' respectively.

The Suspects

Marc Dutroux

One of the earliest suspects to appear on the police's radar was notorious serial killer Marc Dutroux. Known to have operated in the province of Hainaut, of which Mons is the capital, he was responsible for kidnapping six underage girls and keeping them confined to an underground location where they were subjected to vicious kinds of torture. Two of them were found murdered. When he was caught, Dutroux maintained that he was acting at the behest of certain members of the Belgian elite that may have been linked to a high-profile pedophile ring.

Despite being active around Hainaut and full of vicious and violent tendencies, the fact that he was known to prey upon young and underage girls ruled him out as being the Butcher of

Mons. The victims found in the garbage bags were all older, with the youngest of them being 21 years of age.

Smail Tulja

Years before the remains of Carmelina Russo were found, and miles and miles away across the Atlantic Ocean, New York City witnessed firsthand the kind of grisly crimes that Belgium came to know in 1996. A woman discovered a black garbage bag close to the Brooklyn Navy Yard on September 15, 1990, and was shocked to see that it was leaking blood. Once the police arrived at the scene, the bag was checked by Detective Ken Whalen of the 84th Precinct and was found to contain two arms and one leg, presumably those of a woman. But that wasn't the end of it. Another bag was found hours later containing the torso of a woman.

During the investigations, Detective Whalen received a tip that the remains found in the garbage bags belonged to a missing woman named Mary Beal, who lived near Mosholu Parkway. The 61-year-old lived all by herself in a cramped apartment with several dogs, and was reported missing by her neighbors after noticing she hadn't been coming out for her routine morning walks.

Beal was a part-time court translator who spoke a few languages, including Serbo-Croatian. It emerged during the investigation that she was working on a custody battle involving a couple of Yugoslavians living in the city. The man, named Smajo Dzurlic, aka Smail Tulja, was said to be romantically involved with Beal and had fled the United States after her remains were found. Evidence revealed that Tulja had been dating Beal when he was living in New York, which caused resentment in Tulja's wife, who had left messages on Beal's answering machine threatening her. Tulja's apartment in the Bronx also painted a sordid picture as several bloodstains were found there. Who else could they have belonged to but Beal?

Smail Tulja was arrested in 2009 by the Montenegro police, who had teamed up with American police officials. Apparently, Tulja was responsible for a string of murders not just in the U.S. but also in other European countries such as Albania, Montenegro, and Belgium. He was charged with the murder of Mary Beal in the U.S., as well as his wife, who disappeared in Albania several years before his arrest.

Was Smail Tulja the Butcher of Mons? Though he died in prison in 2012, one thing is for certain — after fleeing the U.S. following Beal's murder, Tulja ultimately ended up in the Belgian city of Mons, and was living there when Russo, Bohn, Leclercq, Godart, and Valencia ended up in garbage bags, piece by piece.

Jacques Antoine

Jacques Antoine, a doctor, was accused of being the Butcher of Mons by his son in letters sent to the French police. He based these accusations on the fact that they had been living in Mons at the time of the murders, and he had seen his father carrying black garbage bags around the town. However, the same letters also put holes in the theory as the son continuously wrote about his father's love of guns. So far, there has been no evidence that the Butcher has ever used firearms of any kind in his killings. Nevertheless, in 2012, Antoine was arrested in Strasbourg, France, on the charge of assaulting a woman shortly after his son's letters were sent to the police.

John Sweeney

British citizen John Sweeney also emerged as a suspect based on the fact that he had been convicted in 2011 for the murder of two women by methods that shared the characteristics of the Butcher's victims. Thirty-three-year-old Melissa Halstead had been killed and hacked to pieces in Amsterdam in 1990, and then dumped in the Amstel River. Then, in 2000, 31-year-old Paula Fields was murdered in London. Gaining the moniker of the "Canal Murderer," Sweeney received a life sentence. It is unclear if Sweeney had been in Mons between the murders of Halstead and Fields.

The Butcher of Mons joins the ranks of some of the most terrifying murderers, including the insane Brabant Killers and the sickening Marc Dutroux. But he will remain even more sinister considering there has been no face to associate with him, and perhaps there never will be. Just another man in the crowd, walking and stalking, ready to pick off his next victim.

9

THE TEXAS KILLING FIELDS

Desolation haunts the fields outside League City, a small town nestled between Houston and Galveston, Texas. Surrounded by nothing more than dirt roads and oil rigs, not a soul seems to reside in the 25-acre stretch of land. But though there is no life, there is undoubtedly death in these parts, where nearly 30 bodies have been found since the 1970s.

The Victims

On this eerie patch of dirt-filled land, the bodies of four women were discovered between 1984 and 1991, all of them naked and under trees at a distance of a thousand feet from each other. It would appear as though the victims had been bound at these locations, used by a vicious serial killer as his own personal graveyard. The killer may have kept the women there in those exact spots in order to move between them easily, like a collector checking on his most prized possessions.

But even before then, the fields have been churning out bodies one after the other since the summer of 1971 and as recently as 2006. To date, nearly 30 women have been found in these fields, keeping people from the surrounding towns and communities as far away as possible. And while some of the other women who have been identified have received some closure in the form of convictions, the four women found during the seven years spanning from 1984 to 1991 are still regarded as cold cases, perhaps never to find justice.

Heide Villareal Fye

The Killing Fields would remain relatively undisturbed until April 1984, when a dog unearthed the bones of a human being. Once the police were able to extract the dental records of the corpse, they learned the body belonged to 25-year-old cocktail waitress Heide Fye, who had gone missing on October 10, 1983. She left her parents' house and was heading to Houston by hitchhiking. She had planned to meet her boyfriend there but no one ever heard from her again.

Laura Miller

Later in the year, Laura Miller vanished on September 24, 1984. She and her family had moved to League City only recently, and Laura went with her mother in their car to visit a store nearby as their house was not yet equipped with a telephone. Miller had gone to use the store's payphone to call her boyfriend and was planning to walk the few blocks back home. But she never made it.

According to press reports, it was a coincidence that the Millers lived in close proximity to Heide Fye. Not only that, both girls used to visit the same convenience store from where Miller had disappeared. This was too much of a coincidence for Laura's father, Tim Miller, and he requested the police search for his daughter at the fields along Calder Road — the same fields where Heide Fye's remains had been unearthed only a few months earlier.

The police, however, were of the belief that Fye had run off due to her own personal problems. Laura Miller was a talented young musician, but she was suffering with seizures, which meant she had to miss school for extended periods of time. This may have depressed Laura further, as it meant she could no longer be a part of the school choir. The police reassured Tim Miller and his family that Laura would indeed return or at least call to let them know of her whereabouts.

Since the police never ventured to the fields themselves, it wasn't until 1986 that two dirt bikers came upon the body of a girl later to be known as Jane Doe. This prompted the police to finally search the area where, aside from Jane Doe, they discovered the body of a third girl whose dental records were a perfect match.

It was Laura Miller. She had been buried in the same field close to where Heide Fye was found.

Audrey Lee Cook AKA Jane Doe

The body of Laura Miller wouldn't have been found in the first place were it not for the discovery of another. The two dirt bikers found the body of a woman in the fields in 1986 that could not be identified at that time. She was thus labeled as Jane

Doe for well over three decades until forensic science was able to reveal the identity of not just Jane Doe, but a fourth corpse that would be found in the fields in 1991.

Jane Doe was discovered to be Audrey Lee Cook, a former resident of Tennessee who had been working as a mechanic in several places in Texas such as Houston, Channelview, and Heights until her disappearance in December 1985.

Donna Gonsoulin Prudhomme AKA Janet Doe

Along with Cook's corpse, a fourth body also awaited identification all through the years. Five years after Cook's body was found in the fields, a horseback rider came upon a fourth body in 1991. Labeled as Janet Doe at the time due to a lack of identification, her identity was eventually revealed as Donna Gonsoulin Prudhomme. She was last heard from by her sister Dianne Gonsoulin-Hastings in 1989, when Donna had asked for a copy of her birth certificate in order to travel.

Before her disappearance, Donna had moved to Clear Lake, Texas, along with her two sons from a previous marriage that ended due to abuse. She had entered into a new relationship around the late 1980s, but that didn't last long. By all accounts, Donna had faced several hardships but did her best to provide the best upbringing she could for her children. Upon her disappearance in 1989, all efforts by her family to trace her were in vain. Her children grew up without getting to know her and her eldest son died before the police could identify her corpse.

The Investigation

The murderer of Heide Villareal Fye, Laura Miller, Audrey Lee Cook, and Donna Gonsoulin Prudhomme is unknown and remains at large. With League City's limited resources preventing the effectiveness of conducting such a monumental investigation, the services of the FBI have been enlisted, and they remain open cases with the bureau. It was thanks to the FBI's forensic analysis that the identities of Audrey Lee Cook and Donna Gonsoulin Prudhomme, formerly known as Jane Doe and Janet Doe, respectively, were discovered.

The Behavioral Science Unit of the FBI has created a detailed profile of the man responsible for the above deaths. Based on this profile, the killer is highly organized and possesses the superior intelligence needed to plan, research, and carry out his intentions, as well as effectively avoid detection by the authorities and the public at large. This has led the FBI to believe that the killer is quite adept at blending into a crowd and may just be one of the many residents living in League City or the surrounding towns that no one would even think to suspect. The killer is quite familiar with the territory and could have easily abducted the girls without anyone noticing as he took them to the fields to meet their grisly fate.

The Suspect

Based on this profile, Tim Miller — the father of Laura Miller — was convinced that the killer was none other than local resident Robert Abel. A former NASA engineer turned business owner, Abel leased the land right next to the killing field for his horseback-riding business. It was one of the horseback riders that came upon the body of Donna Gonsoulin Prudhomme in 1991.

Furthermore, Abel's second ex-wife told the police that he had a nasty temper. Though he had never gotten physical with her, she claimed he would beat his horses and livestock with pipes and chains. Abel would also allegedly leave the house for a week or so after an argument with her, and would keep pictures of nude women in his desk drawer. He was also known to leave the rotting corpses of dead livestock out in the open to let the scavengers and carrion birds dispose of them. Such claims were confirmed by Abel's first wife, along with the statement that Abel had threatened to kill her for denying him sex. Abel was married to his first wife for only 41 days.

But despite an extensive search of Abel's property by the police, no evidence or trace to the victims could be found. The only thing that linked him to the crime was a collection of newspaper clippings related to the bodies found at the Texas Killing Fields. But this, along with the claims made by his ex-wives, were all dismissed. Nevertheless, Tim Miller remains adamant of Abel's involvement even to this day, and the former NASA engineer lives a pariah-like existence.

The Aftermath

Since the 1990s, the area around the fields has seen several changes, including a paved road and a neighboring housing development. The land now belongs to a church, and memorials have been put up to honor the women who were found there. Tim Miller has even planted wooden crosses at the locations where the four victims were discovered from 1984 to 1991, including his 16-year-old daughter Laura Miller. There are even plans to build a small park in remembrance of the lives that were taken there.

But while they may be transformed into something that would breed life, the Killing Fields of Texas will always be remembered as full of death. And that blight will not be cleansed away anytime soon.

10

THE 300 (HIGHWAY SERIAL KILLERS)

C ases of a sole serial killer operating in a particular area have proven to be a handful for law enforcement agencies, but a number as high as 300 across the entire United States is astounding. How can such a mammoth number of serial killers operate so effectively? The answer: Because they can do it on the job. Criss-crossing along the various highways and interstates, the Highway Serial Killers travel across towns, cities, and states, leaving a trail of dead bodies in their wake. And they have the advantage of blending into the traffic thanks to their mighty 18-wheel alibis.

The Pattern

In 2004, the bodies of murdered women started popping up along Interstate 40, linking Oklahoma, Texas, Arkansas, and Mississippi. When this pattern was discovered, more and more women's bodies were identified as being dumped near highways. This prompted the F.B.I. to launch the Highway Serial Killings Initiative. Formed not just to coordinate the efforts of various state-based law enforcement agencies to solve these murders, but also to raise awareness among the general public about the victims and circumstances in which such murders may have occurred.

The Victims

Like many victims that fall prey to the wrath of serial killers, the bodies being found along the highways of the U.S. mostly came from a history of drug abuse and prostitution — people who had been drifting around the country from one place to another in pursuit of the next high. Other victims could also include motorists stranded along the highway due to mechanical problems, or hitchhikers looking for an easy ride. Considering the long journeys carried out by truck drivers, women living a high-risk lifestyle involving drugs and prostitution would be a regular feature of truck stops, service stations, and even motels to provide the weary long-haul drivers some instant gratification, and the women enough cash to indulge in their various vices.

Living such a life is already fraught with danger considering the risk of rape, sexual assault, and violence, but it's still shocking to know how many of these individuals end up dead on the various highways of the United States. More than 750 of them in fact, and often enough, the victims are murdered within the 18-wheel trucks themselves and are carried around from state to state until they can be discarded miles away from where they were picked up. This leaves little chance for witnesses or forensic evidence and even creates legal disputes considering the jurisdiction of where the women were abducted, where they were killed, and where they were dumped.

The Murder of Regina Walters

Around the end of 1989, the decomposed body of 14-year-old Regina Walters was discovered in a barn in rural Illinois. A runaway from Pasadena, Texas, Walters was strangled with baling wire and left abandoned in the same barn. A month after her disappearance, her father started receiving anonymous phone calls that were traced back to Oklahoma City and Ennis, Texas. In the phone calls, the sinister voice would talk about Regina Walters and tell her father about how he had made changes to her by cutting her hair.

But how did the 14-year-old from Texas end up in a barn in Illinois in the first place? And how did the killer come to have her home phone number?

The Arrest of Robert Ben Rhoades

Five months after Walters' body was found in Illinois, a state trooper came upon a truck parked dangerously with its hazard lights blinking on Interstate 40, close to Phoenix, Arizona. Upon checking the cab, he found a woman shackled in the truck with cuts on her mouth and welts on her body. Shockingly, a horse bridle was placed around her neck. With all the clear signs of violence, it was a miracle the woman was even alive.

The man responsible for this inhumane treatment was Robert Ben Rhoades, who was arrested at the scene in April 1990. The woman claimed Rhoades had been torturing women like this for 15 years in his truck cab while driving along the American highways. At least, that was what she was told by him.

A long-haul trucker from Houston, Texas, Rhoades was found in possession of all kinds of items of torture, including handcuffs, whips, leashes, alligator clips, dildos, bondage magazines, and blood-soaked towels. And the most damning article of all: a notebook belonging to Regina Walters, with her father's phone number in it. This prompted the authorities to track his movements on the dates of the phone calls received by Walters' father, revealing that Rhoades was indeed in Oklahoma City and Ennis, Texas at the time of the calls.

As if the notebook and phone calls weren't evidence enough, the last piece of shocking evidence was a photograph found of Regina Walters, taken in what appears to be the same barn where she was abandoned. Wearing a knee-length short dress and leather heels, Regina Walters is seen holding her hands up as if she is keeping her attacker at bay, her ashen-white face pleading for mercy. It was enough for Rhoades to be found guilty of Walters' murder and receive a life sentence without parole in the State of Illinois.

But Walters was not the first, and she most certainly was not the last.

The Murdered Newlyweds

In March 2012, Rhoades was transferred to Ozona, Texas, to stand trial for the murder of Douglas Zyskowski and Patricia

Walsh in 1990. D.N.A. evidence had linked Rhoades with the bodies of Zyskowski and Walsh, which were found months apart in 1990 in different locations. It emerged that Zyskowski and Walsh were newlyweds who were hitchhiking to Georgia from Seattle when they were picked up by Rhoades around El Paso. That was the last anyone ever heard of them, and in January, Zyskowski's body was discovered along Interstate 10 near Ozona. About ten months later, the body of Walsh was found in Utah by some deer hunters. And while it took two years to identify the first body as Zyskowski, Walsh's corpse remained unidentified for 13 years until her dental records returned an appropriate match.

The Drop In The Ocean

Rhoades is just one, but there are another 300 Highway Serial Killers cruising along the interstates with not a care in the world as they mercilessly abduct, rape, torture, and kill their victims, eventually dumping them by the miles upon miles of endless concrete and asphalt. They carry their crime scenes, their instruments of torture, and their victims along wherever they go and leave virtually no trace of D.N.A. or evidence behind to match with any fixed location.

The Arrest of John Robert Williams

In 2004, the Oklahoma Bureau of Investigation approached the F.B.I. for assistance in the cases of seven killings, the bodies of which were found along various roadsides of I-40. All of the victims were women, primarily working as sex workers at truck stops. With the help of the F.B.I., the victims were cross-referenced with another 250 cases of female victims found at roadsides and with similar patterns. Ultimately, the killer was found by complete fluke.

Late that year, police in Mississippi received a call from a woman claiming that she and her boyfriend had come upon the body of a woman near a rural county road. During the investigation and questioning of both the woman and the boyfriend, the police were able to determine that it was the pair who were responsible for the murder. Both were arrested, and the man confessed to over 12 other such killings, including some that were being investigated by the Oklahoma Bureau of Investigation.

The man, a 28-year-old truck driver named John Robert Williams, also confessed to the methods and details of the murders, such as strangulations or by using a ligature. He claimed to have committed sexual assaults on his victims as well, both before and after their deaths. The reason his girlfriend called the police about 'finding' the woman in Mississippi was because they feared they had been seen leaving with her from a casino. But further investigations have not yielded any D.N.A. matching Williams with the samples found upon the victims, and Williams himself has recanted his confession.

Nevertheless, the claims made in his confession were quite detailed, particularly regarding those of a victim named Buffie Rae Brawley. For instance, Williams stated that Brawley was a truck stop sex worker who had approached him for sex while he was in his truck. He was aware that Brawley had a tattoo of the word 'Ebony' on her right thigh, though that could have been known to the locals. But his other claims of the state of the body could only have been known by the murderer. Williams claimed that Brawley had deep lacerations on her head that were inflicted by a tire thumper.

Williams also made more bold claims in the case of Brawley. According to one investigator, he said that "the second she (Brawley) tapped on my window, she was a dead woman." With regards to the lack of D.N.A. evidence, an investigator from Texas revealed that during an interview, Williams "actually bragged that we wouldn't find any D.N.A. because he didn't have sex with them in the traditional sense." The police department in Grapevine, Texas, has submitted a potential death penalty case for Williams to the DA.

The Legs from Vegas

In 2005, some ATV riders came across a pair of human legs in some woods near the I-55 in central Illinois. In a decomposing state, the only identifying things about the legs were the painted toenails and a partial tattoo. With the help of the F.B.I., the state police were able to link the tattoo three years later to Lindsay Harris. A call girl by trade, the 21-year old Harris, had gone missing about two weeks before the riders found her legs. But while her legs were found in Illinois, Harris had vanished from the Las Vegas strip, a distance of nearly 1400 miles. As she was one of four such sex workers who went missing from 2003 to 2005, the authorities concluded that the murderer was likely a truck driver or someone who traveled quite frequently on the I-55 as it correlated to the patterns collected in the F.B.I. database.

The Arrest of Bruce Mendenhall

In July 2007, truck driver Bruce Mendenhall was arrested outside a truck stop near East Nashville, Tennessee. The arresting officer was a veteran homicide investigator with the Nashville Police Department, Sgt. Pat Postiglione, who had been investigating the murder of a woman named Sara Hulbert. A sex worker, Hulbert's body was found behind the same truck stop. Postiglione came upon Mendenhall as a possible suspect after reviewing the camera footage of the truck stop where Hulbert was found. Considering that there was a never-ending inflow and outflow of trucks from that stop, it was only by chance that Postiglione noticed a yellow 18-wheeler coming and going in just 30 minutes. Considering that most truck drivers would stay at the stops for at least an hour to refuel their trucks and eat or even sleep, Postiglione thought to check it out.

When he arrived at the truck stop the following day, Postiglione got lucky when he spotted a yellow truck heading towards East Nashville. Known for being an area frequented by sex workers, Postiglione followed the 18-wheeler as it drove through several streets before finally stopping at the truck stop. As Postiglione got the driver, Bruce Mendenhall, to step out of the cab, he noticed that Bruce had a speck of blood on his thumb, and other drops on the driver's door. Instinctively, he decided that he needed to search the truck, and Mendenhall even voluntarily signed a consent form for the search and agreed to a D.N.A. swab.

Upon searching the truck cab, Postiglione found a plastic bag with bloodied women's clothing, as well as a cell phone and A.T.M. card that belonged to another missing woman. Further analysis of the cab by the Crime Scene Investigators revealed blood and D.N.A. that connected Mendenhall to at least seven other victims. Mendenhall was convicted of Sara Hulbert's murder in 2010 and has also been charged with three other murders. His appeal was rejected in 2017, and he is still under investigation for other unsolved murders.

The Arrest of Adam Leroy Lane

A bizarre occurrence that took place a month after the arrest of Mendenhall saw a truck driver break pattern. In the Boston suburbs, Adam Leroy Lane was found attempting to assault 15-year-old Shea McDonough in her bedroom when he was caught and subdued by the girl's father, Kevin McDonough. He and his wife Jeannie went to their daughter's bedroom late at night, then they heard a whimper and found Shea being held at knife-point by a masked intruder.

After the police arrived, Lane's big rig was found parked outside the McDonough's house, which marked the first time that a truck driver had targeted someone who was not a sex worker, nor was she on an interstate or at a truck-stop. Upon searching his truck, the police discovered a DVD about a serial killer. Lane himself was armed with three other knives, a throwing star, and a length of wire. A message was sent to the F.B.I. to investigate Lane for possible criminal activity as part of the Highway Serial Killings Initiative, which found Lane linked to more killings in 2 other states. Lane was convicted after pleading guilty to avoid the death penalty and is serving a 50-year sentence.

The Final Frontier

Such killers have been prowling unabated since the 1950s when the U.S. government completed work on the Interstate System. They have found the freedom of the open road their domain, and with the varying laws of each state and town, it is years before they are even suspected. With over a thousand local law enforcement agencies in Texas alone — including sheriff's offices, police departments, and Texas Rangers — maintaining a centralized database of highway disappearances and dead bodies becomes a daunting task, let alone coordination with agencies in other states.

Furthermore, even the F.B.I.'s Highway Serial Killings initiative may not have an accurate number of actual victims being reported, as all information provided to the bureau by state agencies is voluntary. More than 750 victims have been added to the databases of bodies found on the endless highways, but even 750 may just be the tip of the iceberg.

Until law enforcement agencies can develop better security and surveillance of the highway networks, there is no telling just how many women are being shuttled across the country in 18-wheelers, and what agonies they must be suffering as their screams are lost amidst the vacuum of the open road.

CONCLUSION

Do we ever notice the ones that are truly the most dangerous? One may never know just what waits around the corner. It's likely best that we never find out, unlike the victims mentioned in these pages who had lost their way. Or others who wanted nothing more than to ensure the well-being of their children, to belong, and to be loved.

It is only by a twist of fate that you are getting to read about these stories rather than being featured in them. Now, it's your turn to spread the news. To spread the knowledge of the horrors that could await countless others — like Laura Miller, Martine Bohn, Wilhelm Friedrich Horst Meyer, Jens Uwe Rusch, Lena Sharpe, Jose Vanden Eynde, Hazel Lewis, Souvik Pal, Helen Barthelemy, Jae Stevens, and who knows how many others like them who remain on the fringe of society or seek the next best thrill.

The more you know, the more you can let others know of the horrors that befell these poor lost souls. And the more you spread the word, the more cautious you will make them of the people they may never have suspected until now.

And who knows. Maybe you will stumble upon a killer sequestered in your own neighborhood one day. Let's just hope that when you do, it's not too late.

REFERENCES

Ahmed, A., Rozas, A. R., Haggerty, R., & Woodward, W. (2007, November 16). 1st murder victim identified. Chicagotribune.com. https://www.chicagotribune.com/news/ct-xpm-2007-11-16-0711150975-story.html

BBC. (2013, October 31). Souvik Pal: Manchester student canal death "a mystery." BBC News. https://www.bbc.com/news/uk-england-manchester-24743615

BBC. (2020, June 9). Chicago sees deadliest day in decades amid protests and curfew. BBC News. https://www.bbc.com/news/world-us-canada-52984535

Belgian police release photo in bid to crack "Brabant Killers" case. (2020, June 16). The Guardian. https://www.theguardian.com/world/2020/jun/16/belgian-police-release-photo-in-bid-to-crack-crazy-brabant-killers-case

Bevan, R. (2019, January 3). Jack the Stripper and the Hammersmith murders. Crime + Investigation. https://www. crimeandinvestigation.co.uk/article/jack-the-stripper-and-the-hammersmith-murders

Box, D. (2018, September 5). Manchester Pusher: Does a serial killer haunt the city's canals? BBC News. https://www.bbc. com/news/uk-england-manchester-45173888

Brown, B. (2020, April 17). Myths of Manchester: The Canal Pusher. Manchester's Finest. https://www.manchestersfinest. com/articles/myths-manchester-canal-pusher/

Coon, D. R. (2012). Sun, Sand, and Citizenship: The Marketing of Gay Tourism. Journal of Homosexuality, 59(4), 511–534. https://doi.org/10.1080/00918369.2012.648883

Dall'Armellina, V. (2014, October 25). Police Are Running Out of Time to Catch the "Crazy Brabant Killers." Www.vice.com. https://www.vice.com/en/article/59aekd/ police-are-running-out-of-time-to-catch-the-crazy-brabant-killers

Davis, M. (2013, September 3). Lost Stockport reveller sent text to girlfriend minutes before he drowned. Manchester Evening News. https://www.manchestereveningnews.co.uk/news/ greater-manchester-news/michael-simpson-22-heaton-norris-5832528

FBI. (2009, April 6). Highway Serial Killings Initiative. FBI. https://archives.fbi.gov/archives/news/stories/2009/april/highwayserial_040609

FBI. (2019). The Killing Fields | Federal Bureau of Investigation. Federal Bureau of Investigation. https://www.fbi. gov/news/stories/seeking-information-in-unsolved-killing-fields-murders-091819

Figueroa, A. S. and A. (2018, January 16). 75 women have been strangled or smothered in Chicago since 2001. Most of their killers got away. Chicagotribune.com. https://www. chicagotribune.com/news/breaking/ct-met-chicago-women-strangled-20180103-story.html

Flynn, M. (2019, April 17). Bodies found in the "killing fields" haunted Southeast Texas for decades. Will new clues lead to a suspect?. Washington Post. https://www.washingtonpost.com/nation/2019/04/17/bodies-found-killing-fields-haunted-southeast-texas-decades-will-new-clues-lead-suspect/

Glendinning, A. (2015a, August 25). Manchester canal pusher: GMP rubbish serial killer claims saying there is nothing linking the deaths. Manchester Evening News. https://www. manchestereveningnews.co.uk/news/greater-manchester-news/manchester-canal-pusher-gmp-deny-9924534

Glendinning, A. (2015b, August 25). "The Manchester Pusher is real": Author claims there is a serial killer stalking city's canals. Manchester Evening News. https://www.

manchestereveningnews.co.uk/news/manchester-canal-pusher-serial-killer-9924431

Glover, S. (2009, April 5). FBI makes a connection between long-haul truckers, serial killings. Los Angeles Times. https://www.latimes.com/archives/la-xpm-2009-apr-05-me-serialkillers5-story.html

Green, E. (2014, December 11). The Untold Story of the Doodler Murders. The Awl. https://www.theawl.com/2014/12/the-untold-story-of-the-doodler-murders/

Hannaford, A. (2012, November 7). Texas leads the nation in unsolved serial highway homicides. The Texas Observer. https://www.texasobserver.org/highway-injustice/

Hawken, A. (2019, February 11). Serial killer Jack The Stripper who murdered six women in London "was metalworker who slaughtered two young girls 43 years earlier." The Sun. https://www.thesun.co.uk/news/8402525/jack-stripper-murdered-six-women-london/

Hesketh, S. (2015, January 11). Manchester's KILLER canals: Fears of "serial slayer" as 61 people die in city waterways. Dailystar.co.uk. https://www.dailystar.co.uk/news/latest-news/sixty-one-people-died-mysteriously-17330488

Hewitt, L. (2015, May 7). Jack the Stripper: Hammersmith Nude Murders. Historic Mysteries. https://www.historicmysteries.com/jack-the-stripper/

Hollandsworth, S. (1999, October 1). Is Robert Abel Getting Away With Murder? Texas Monthly. https://www.texasmonthly.com/articles/is-robert-abel-getting-away-with-murder/

Hope, A. (2020, June 16). Brabant Killers case in Belgium: who, what, when? The Brussels Times. https://www.brusselstimes.com/news/belgium-all-news/117044/brabant-killers-case-in-belgium-who-what-when/

Hunter, B. (2019, April 27). CRIME HUNTER: Two serial killers preying on Chicago sex workers? Torontosun. https://torontosun.com/news/world/crime-hunter-two-serial-killers-preying-on-chicago-sex-workers

Is There an Active Serial Killer in Chicago? (2019, May 27). The Murder Squad. http://themurdersquad.com/episodes/is-there-an-active-serial-killer-in-chicago/

Janos, A. (2018, June 18). Is There a Serial Killer in Chicago Right Now, Strangling Women and Burning Their Bodies? A&E. https://www.aetv.com/real-crime/is-there-a-serial-killer-in-chicago-right-now-strangling-women-and-burning-their-bodies

Janos, A. (2021, January 8). Who Was Jack the Stripper? A&E. https://www.aetv.com/real-crime/jack-the-stripper

Johnson, H. (2013, February 5). Death of Stone Roses fan to remain a mystery. Manchester Evening News. https://www.

manchestereveningnews.co.uk/news/parents-told-son-chris-brahneys-1293081

Johnston, L. (2020, September 11). The Unsolved Atlanta Ripper Case. Medium. https://medium.com/the-true-crime-edition/the-unsolved-atlanta-ripper-case-2e9e73c67ef1

McMaster, K. (2018, August 15). The Monster of Florence. Mysite. https://www.truecrimepress.com/post/the-monster-of-florence

Monster of Florence. (n.d.). Florence Web Guide. Retrieved April 25, 2021, from http://www.florencewebguide.com/monster-of-florence.html

Murders, U. (2004, April 17). David Plunkett - Unsolved Murder 2004 - Manchester Ship Canal, Manchester. UnsolvedMurders.co.uk. http://www.unsolved-murders.co.uk/murder-content.php?key=170&termRef=David%20Plunkett

Murders, U. (2010, December 17). Nathan Tomlinson - Unsolved Murder 2010 - River Irwell. UnsolvedMurders.co.uk. http://www.unsolved-murders.co.uk/murder-content.php?key=2850&termRef=Nathan%20Tomlinson

Napolitano, A. (2018, July 11). 10 Eerie Facts About The Monster Of Florence. Listverse. https://listverse.com/2018/07/11/10-eerie-facts-about-the-monster-of-florence/

Olsen, M. B. (2018, April 15). Cyclist's near death experience reignites fears of a "Manchester canal pusher." Metro. https://

metro.co.uk/2018/04/15/cyclists-near-death-experience-reignites-fears-of-a-manchester-canal-pusher-serial-killer-7469258/

Portraits of Life: Hazel Lewis. (2020, December 29). Unforgotten 51. https://www.unforgotten51.com/2020/12/portraits-of-life-hazel-lewis.html

Portraits of Life: Theresa Bunn. (2020, December 29). Unforgotten 51. https://www.unforgotten51.com/2020/12/portraits-of-life-theresa-bunn.html#more

Sadler, B. (1996, February 13). CNN - So-called "monster" acquitted - Feb. 13, 1996. Edition.cnn.com. http://edition.cnn.com/WORLD/9602/italy_florence/

Scheerhout, J. (2018, June 6). "The Manchester Pusher": Relatives of canal death victims raise claims of serial killer in TV documentary. Manchester Evening News. https://www.manchestereveningnews.co.uk/news/greater-manchester-news/manchester-pusher-canal-deaths-claim-10742451

Scheerhout, J. (2020, January 12). Why do people still believe The Pusher is real? Manchester Evening News. https://www.manchestereveningnews.co.uk/news/greater-manchester-news/people-still-believe-pusher-real-17533335

Sege, B. A. (2013, May 21). Cops seek to identify body in burned trash bin. Chicagotribune.com. https://www.

chicagotribune.com/news/breaking/chi-burned-body-found-in-logan-square-dumpster-20130520-story.html

staffostello. (2020, August 7). Inquiry on the Zodiac-Monster of Florence connection. Mostro Di Firenze. https://ostellovolante. com/2020/08/07/inquiry-on-the-zodiac-monster-of-florence-connection-by-francesco-amicone-may-19-2018/

Sweeney, A. (2019, May 14). Chicago police are taking a new look at the unsolved slayings of 55 women — and the possibility a serial killer is involved. Chicagotribune.com. https://www. chicagotribune.com/news/breaking/ct-met-strangled-women-chicago-police-task-force-20190510-story.html

Swinging 60s - Capital of Cool. (n.d.). Sky HISTORY TV Channel. Retrieved April 25, 2021, from https://www.history. co.uk/history-of-london/swinging-60s-capital-of-cool#:~:text=For%20a%20few%20years%20in

The Doodler. (2015, March 30). The Lost and Found. https:// cryptail.wordpress.com/the-doodler/

The Hammersmith Murders | History Blog UK. (2021, January 28). Www.theministryofhistory.co.uk. https://www. theministryofhistory.co.uk/short-histories-blog/hammersmith-jack-the-stripper-murders

The Monster of Florence. (2015, February 16). Murder Is Everywhere. https://murderiseverywhere.blogspot.com/2015/ 02/the-monster-of-florence.html

Tingle, R. (2019, February 11). New documentary identifies Jack The Stripper as a Welsh panel beater. Mail Online. https://www.dailymail.co.uk/news/article-6690567/New-documentary-identifies-Jack-Stripper-Welsh-panel-beater.html

Tribune, C. (2007, November 26). Family remembers 2nd victim as giving. Chicagotribune.com. https://www.chicagotribune.com/news/ct-xpm-2007-11-26-0711260430-story.html

Tucker, D. (2019, April 16). A Serial Killer May Be Preying On Black Women In Chicago. WBEZ Chicago. https://www.wbez.org/stories/a-serial-killer-may-be-preying-on-black-women-in-chicago/21b45020-ca53-490e-8efe-b9c6ebbe11f3

Unsplash. (n.d.-a). Photo by Ali Kazal on Unsplash. Unsplash.com. Retrieved April 25, 2021, from https://unsplash.com/photos/QKCo0sBAm58

Unsplash. (n.d.-b). Photo by Bernardo Lorena Ponte on Unsplash. Unsplash.com. Retrieved April 25, 2021, from https://unsplash.com/photos/_YjFrAxyYxg

Unsplash. (n.d.-c). Photo by Chris Rhoads on Unsplash. Unsplash.com. Retrieved April 25, 2021, from https://unsplash.com/photos/XGMF6N-u6rg

Unsplash. (n.d.-d). Photo by Edward Howell on Unsplash. Unsplash.com. Retrieved April 25, 2021, from https://unsplash.com/photos/xqoco1z7mow

Unsplash. (n.d.-e). Photo by Emiliano Vittoriosi on Unsplash. Unsplash.com. https://unsplash.com/photos/-7Z5tLMcFAQ

Unsplash. (n.d.-f). Photo by Eva Dang on Unsplash. Unsplash.com. Retrieved April 25, 2021, from https://unsplash.com/photos/EXdXLrZXS9Q

Unsplash. (n.d.-g). Photo by Giannis Skarlatos on Unsplash. Unsplash.com. Retrieved April 25, 2021, from https://unsplash.com/photos/eRZlk7vYNl4

Unsplash. (n.d.-h). Photo by Jack Gibson on Unsplash. Unsplash.com. Retrieved April 25, 2021, from https://unsplash.com/photos/vt8zaknCdes

Unsplash. (n.d.-i). Photo by Jay Heike on Unsplash. Unsplash.com. Retrieved April 25, 2021, from https://unsplash.com/photos/1HgkwxaPkE8

Unsplash. (n.d.-j). Photo by Jonathan Cosens Photography on Unsplash. Unsplash.com. Retrieved April 25, 2021, from https://unsplash.com/photos/vW8LpqbviCE

Unsplash. (n.d.-k). Photo by Joshua Case on Unsplash. Unsplash.com. Retrieved April 25, 2021, from https://unsplash.com/photos/ThQF0WEp2tM

Unsplash. (n.d.-l). Photo by Louis Cheng on Unsplash. Unsplash.com. Retrieved April 25, 2021, from https://unsplash.com/photos/HR9As7ZZ06Y

Unsplash. (n.d.-m). Photo by Markus Spiske on Unsplash. Unsplash.com. Retrieved April 25, 2021, from https://unsplash.com/photos/eioMwO2IJ2E

Unsplash. (n.d.-n). Photo by Max Templeton on Unsplash. Unsplash.com. Retrieved April 25, 2021, from https://unsplash.com/photos/DkYF2DF9MWQ

Unsplash. (n.d.-o). Photo by Meriç Dağlı on Unsplash. Unsplash.com. Retrieved April 25, 2021, from https://unsplash.com/photos/DtCEcY1k_qE

Unsplash. (n.d.-p). Photo by Neal Kharawala on Unsplash. Unsplash.com. Retrieved April 25, 2021, from https://unsplash.com/photos/XXA8PTuLD1Y

Unsplash. (n.d.-q). Photo by Paul Einerhand on Unsplash. Unsplash.com. Retrieved April 25, 2021, from https://unsplash.com/photos/gIp8WnFJrSU

Unsplash. (n.d.-r). Photo by Roberto Blacio on Unsplash. Unsplash.com. Retrieved April 25, 2021, from https://unsplash.com/photos/Zzf1KkNpJyU

Unsplash. (n.d.-s). Photo by Sébastien Lavalaye on Unsplash. Unsplash.com. Retrieved April 25, 2021, from https://unsplash.com/photos/SJX3f5EEpC4

Unsplash. (n.d.-t). Photo by Steven Lewis on Unsplash. Unsplash.com. Retrieved April 25, 2021, from https://unsplash.com/photos/dmHnXJ-5ilQ

Wells, L. (2017, February 15). Court denies appeal from convicted killer Mendenhall. Evansville Courier & Press. https://www.courierpress.com/story/news/crime/2017/02/15/court-denies-appeal-convicted-killer-mendenhall/97942402/

Welton, B. (2018, July 31). 10 Horrifying Facts About The Brabant Killers. Listverse. https://listverse.com/2018/07/31/10-horrifying-facts-about-the-brabant-killers/

Welton, B. (2019, February 12). 10 Gruesome Facts About The Butcher Of Mons. Listverse. https://listverse.com/2019/02/12/10-gruesome-facts-about-the-butcher-of-mons/

Wire, S.-T. (2017, June 23). Woman found strangled in street in East Garfield Park. Chicago Sun-Times. https://chicago.suntimes.com/2017/6/23/18383763/woman-found-strangled-in-street-in-east-garfield-park

MORE FROM D.R. WERNER

For more books and information on D.R. Werner visit

www.drwernerbooks.com

AND

Join the growing true crime facebook group at

www.facebook.com/drwernerbooks

See you there!

Made in the USA
Monee, IL
19 October 2022

16112124R00100